THE
MODERATOR

INSIDE FACEBOOK'S DIRTY WORK
IN IRELAND

CHRIS GRAY

Gill Books

Gill Books
Hume Avenue
Park West
Dublin 12
www.gillbooks.ie

Gill Books is an imprint of M.H. Gill and Co.

Some names and identifying details have been changed to protect the
privacy of the people involved.

9780717192830

Edited by Djinn von Noorden
Proofread by Ruairí Ó Brógáin
Designed by Bartek Janczak
Print origination by O'K Graphic Design, Dublin
Printed by ScandBook AB, Sweden

This book is typeset in 12/18 pt Minion Pro.

A CIP catalogue record for this book is available from the British Library.

5 4 3 2 1

THE MODERATOR

Chris Gray is a former community operations analyst for Facebook. He has lived in a dozen countries around the world and travelled to over 50. He is currently pursuing legal action against his former employers.

CONTENTS

INTRODUCTION

On 4 December 2019 Dave Coleman, one of the leading personal injury lawyers in Ireland, walked into the European headquarters of Facebook, one of the wealthiest and most powerful corporations in the world. In his hand were documents calling them to account for their actions in the High Court. The writ, served on my behalf, detailed the working conditions of the people who look at toxic content so that people like you don't have to and the post-traumatic stress disorders, depression and other mental health issues that the workers deal with as a result.

This book is about more than just a court case, although it's a court case which affects everyone using social media, and everyone living in a society in which social media is a thing. It's about life in the ranks of social media's content moderation army, how the work is done, the structural issues facing the industry, the endless ethical quandaries and semantic arguments and the debilitating effects of 'the drip': daily exposure to gruesome violence, petty squabbles, nasty racist propaganda from small-minded people, suggestively shaped vegetables and unfunny jokes from people whose intention may or may not have been to cause harm.

If you're looking for a recounting of corporate malfeasance or an enquiry into the politics and economics of global content moderation in the world's biggest social media empire, then there is plenty here for you. However, it's also a human story about the good guys, my former colleagues, tens of thousands of decent ordinary people around the world, who are still forced to sit in crowded offices and make decisions about stuff that other people have found offensive or disturbing enough to complain about.

You can share your inspirational memes, cat videos and the best version of yourself online in relative peace and safety because there is a secret army working tirelessly to create a safe space for you to do so. They are content moderators, the internet's police force, and without them your social media would be unusable.

Most content moderators are relegated to the shadows and gagged by non-disclosure agreements (NDAs) – what I call the Facebook omertà – afraid to speak because of what that might mean for their future employment prospects, never mind the fear of being sued. They're not allowed to tell you what goes on in secret – the management by intimidation, the dark laughter, the camaraderie, the surreal arguments about women's bodies, the mental gymnastics, the absurdities, the trauma – so I'll have to do it. It's my job to tell their stories as well as mine, to give them a voice, to make sure the truth is out there.

I have acquired a new set of demons that will probably be with me for life and have taken ownership of experiences I would prefer to have never had. I have had to learn a lot about mental health that I didn't want to and acknowledge my weaknesses and vulnerabilities. Ultimately, it's a book about becoming a better person, overcoming failure and finding redemption.

Along the way, I have become the face of a campaign to reform the working conditions of over 100,000 people worldwide, including the surveillance they're under. I've fought with the Data Protection Commission over their failure to enforce GDPR (the General Data Protection Regulation which regulates how companies protect the personal data of EU citizens). I have been forced to learn to play the game as an activist and consultant to media and politicians, plus find some way to make a living while doing it. I've become an expert, the go-to guy for anyone wanting to understand one of the most vexing problems of our time. This book is also about that eye-opening journey.

This is a book about unpleasantness, mediocrity, compliance, and resistance – all great topics for irreverence. My aim in telling this story is to point out the absurdities, celebrate the fun times and poke fun at those in power as I confront them with the truth.[†]

---

† In the late 1940s, the Superman radio series *Clan of the Fiery Cross* so effectively mocked the Ku Klux Klan that they were unable to recruit new members. The show was based on undercover reporting which revealed the Klan's secrets. People started showing up at their rallies just to make fun of them as the show had destroyed their mystique and exposed them for what they were.

I hope this book can transcend what Hannah Arendt called 'the banality of evil' by having the occasional chuckle at the expense of the corporate culture that has done so much harm to so many people. If we can't laugh at adversity, or call out absurdity for what it is, then how else are we going to cope?

Sometimes there's no way out of a bad situation except to go through it, to minimise it, to find a way to laugh at it, or oneself. It's how I deal with things

My story starts, as so many things in tech start these days, in a coffee shop.

ONE

WHAT COULD POSSIBLY GO WRONG?

I f in March 2019 you had been in the right coffee shop in Dublin, you might have seen a man in a ridiculous hat sitting with a blonde woman and a cold cup of cocoa. He had tears streaming down his cheeks.

That was me. The woman was Jennifer O'Connell, a reporter from the *Irish Times*, and the meeting was supposed to be a simple off-the-record interview about working conditions in one of the world's great companies. I had spent the previous year working as a content moderator, 'watching disturbing things on Facebook so that you don't have to', employed by a company called CPL under contract to Facebook.

Jennifer had got my phone number from someone and wanted to chat. I'm generally an obliging sort of guy so I squeezed her in on the way to Tesco without thinking too much of it. We sat there, me telling amusing stories about characters like James the Frapist or how employees would be 'disappeared' as if they were in some bizarre techno-fascist dictatorship. Everything was fine until she insisted on getting into detail about the disturbing content I had seen.

After years in business education, talking is easy for me. However, this question made me pause. She wanted to talk about feelings, and I grew up believing that boys don't cry. I'm a natural sceptic and was still vaguely contemptuous of 'modern diseases' like PTSD, ADHD, Asperger's and depression. She had already suggested to me that I might have been traumatised by the work and I hadn't wanted to have that conversation. It seemed ridiculous.

This was the first time I had ever discussed my job in detail with anyone and I wasn't prepared for the flood of memories it would release.

I remember staring into space while I gathered my thoughts. There was a moment of silence, of waiting, like I was gazing into a pool of water and trying to figure out what was rising to the surface. Then I saw them – the ghosts – the dead babies, the tortured, the abused, those who died horribly in motor accidents, the murdered, the bullied, the reviled, all those victims we were supposed to protect, all that pain and suffering and evil delight, all waiting to be brought back to life by my words.

I've just looked back at the article Jennifer wrote after that first interview, published in the *Irish Times* on 30 March 2019, and reading it again made me feel physically sick. Not because of any problem I have with the reporting itself; it's because giving life to those ghosts that day released something that, three years later, I still can't always control, even after all the therapy and anti-depressants. I have had to accept that something's not right in my head and that I have a problem.

If I had to sum up my entire experience with Facebook in one word, I would choose 'stupid'. Everything that happened need never have happened if people, including myself, had just made a bit more effort to think things through. I blame myself as much as I blame anyone else. The warning signs were all there from the very beginning, in a Starbucks in Mianyang, a city in Sichuan, Central China, but I didn't take any notice.

I was too busy fretting about everything that could go wrong with my upcoming Skype interview to notice that the people on the other end of the call didn't have things under control. I was there with a friend, and we were testing the Wi-Fi, testing the mobile phone signal, making test calls on Skype to people in Europe and generally doing everything in our power to minimise the technology risk.

Unfortunately, there are two ends to every connection and my interviewers at CPL didn't have everything under control on their end. After 30 minutes of waiting, frantically checking things and shouting 'Can you hear me?' my time slot was over. The interview was a dud, and I was left staring at my phone in disbelief.

I needed this job so I could get back to where I was supposed to be. Since Skype wasn't working, I decided to go for broke. I emailed to set up an in-person interview for the following week, bought myself a ticket to the other side of the world and left a great job in a hurry to pursue the greener grass of modern Ireland.

—

I've had a long, unusual and interesting life and tend to think of myself as a tough world traveller who can cope with anything. I've lived and worked a variety of jobs in a dozen countries. I've been stony broke thousands of miles from home and I have always been fine. I'm a survivor. But this time I was facing a new and daunting challenge: I was trying to get a real job for the first time in my life.

In 2016 I had recently moved to Dublin with my wife, who is from Indonesia, after many years of teaching MBA-level business English in corporations and universities in Asia. She speaks several Asian languages and had no problems finding a job working for a company called CPL under contract to Facebook, which needed linguists to police the global internet and tell them which accounts were real and which were fakes or duplicates. I, however, was struggling to find a job, so while she was starting an exciting new career, I was twiddling my thumbs, haemorrhaging money and getting increasingly desperate.

Eventually, we decided that I should just take off to China, where I have years of experience and all the marketable skills you could ask for. Within ten days of making that decision, I was out in panda country, at a teacher training college in Sichuan, far from home but making money again and relatively stress-free. The plan was to replenish our funds for a few months and apply for jobs from there while my wife stayed in a friend's spare room in Dublin.

I had over 240 students in total. The teaching load was easy, I had complete freedom to design my own course, and

I couldn't walk down the street without some cheerful young person recognising me and calling out, 'Hi, Uncle Chris!' At another time in my life I would have been deliriously happy, but now I was tired of Asia and desperate to get back to my lovely wife. Pleasant as it was, I was just marking time.

I went 'home' for nearly two months over the winter break. On workdays I would get up every morning and walk her to the Facebook office at Number Four, Grand Canal Square (GC4), kiss her goodbye on the steps and be there at the end of the day when she finished. It was quite idyllic. She was excited to be part of the Facebook family, anxious to show her workplace off to me, and me off to her workmates, and a couple of times she was able to bring me into the building as a guest for lunch. I was very impressed. The Facebook brand was mostly untarnished at the time and, like everyone else, I was enamoured of the glamour around big tech. I wasn't allowed into the desk areas, but I saw the common spaces and it was a beautiful work environment. There was lots of wood, open space and natural light all harmoniously arranged to create a feeling of space and possibility. The vibe was positive and happy. CPL contractors seemed to rub shoulders with Facebook's full-time employees in the canteen, and a huge team laboured full-time to produce free, high-quality food in abundance for all. Best of all, there was a sign above the main door that read 'Move fast and break things!' a mantra attributed to Facebook's god-like leader, Mark Zuckerberg, and an inherently optimistic way of working which fit my world-traveller self-image – the guy who can go anywhere and deal with anything. I didn't realise it at the time, in 2017, but Facebook had abandoned this motto some three years earlier in favour of 'Move fast with stable infrastructure'. It's not as catchy and inspirational – it sounds like something dreamt up by the Communist Party of China – but I suppose it projects the kind of maturity and stability appropriate for the darling of the stock exchange. It's just a pity that nobody had told the people in Dublin, who hadn't moved fast enough to replace the old sign yet.

Then one day in May of that year, CPL sent an email to all of their thousands of staff. They had a major hiring campaign happening and needed bums on seats in a hurry, so they were asking their existing workforce for introductions. There had been a recent surge in horrifying content on Facebook or horrifying events linked to content on Facebook, and Zuckerberg had just announced he was increasing the number of people working in content moderation.

I was vaguely aware at this point that Facebook had a problem with some of the stuff that people were putting on Facebook. Even in China, it was impossible not to see the headlines about people live-streaming gruesome acts on Facebook, and the world was also starting to ask questions about harm to society and individuals from some of the messaging on social media. The Cambridge Analytica scandal was just breaking, and it would soon become clear that if you just let everyone say whatever they want online then soon the loudest and nastiest voices would start to take over and propagate narratives the world is better off without.

Facebook had finally decided to take action – or had been pushed into it by criticism from the media and politicians – and were ramping up their content moderation efforts at last. CPL already had 400 people doing Trust and Safety work for Facebook in Dublin, about ten per cent of the global total workforce, and were perfectly placed to take on this expansion. So, they had been asked to find another 400 and double the size of their operation in a hurry.

Trust and Safety, incidentally, is the industry term encapsulating both 'inauthentic behaviour' and content moderation. Safety, my job, can be summed up as dealing with inappropriate content, while Trust is what my wife was focused on. She policed user accounts and identified the fakes, which had been the focus of the T&S effort up to that point. Now the big issue was what people were saying rather than who they were.

It sounded like an interesting and worthwhile challenge even if the money wasn't great, so I jumped at the opportunity to get involved. I thought that this would be my foot in the door, a chance to start a proper career after decades of making it up as I went along. I was in the early days of an industry that was poised for massive growth and would be able to create a role for myself further up the ladder once I was in.

I rewrote my CV as convincingly as possible, spent hours crafting a cover letter and in very short order arranged an online interview for the role of 'Community Operations Analyst' on-site at Facebook. This is how I found myself in a Starbucks in Mianyang, trying to have a Skype call with some CPL recruiter who had apparently never used the technology before, and eventually concluding that I needed to just get to Dublin and present myself in person before the opportunity went away.

So, a week later, after a flurry of emails and a mad dash to get back from China and find a new place for us to live, I pitched up at CPL's head office building, one of those fantastic huge old townhouses on Merrion Square in south Dublin. CPL started life as 'Computer Placement Limited' in 1989, providing staff for the IT industry, which is a polite term for 'running outsourced call centres using cheap labour'. Twenty years later they had 21 offices, plus an unknown number of teams working 'on-site' for clients like Facebook, and the company's shares were listed on the London Stock Exchange. By the time I arrived for my interview, they boasted over 10,000 employees across Europe; the founder, Anne Heraty, was one of the richest people in Ireland; and it seemed only natural that they would operate from a prestigious address like this one.

I don't remember much about the interview, except that it wasn't a very rigorous process. I got the distinct impression that they had a checklist and just needed me to give them the right answers so they could tick the boxes and then plonk me down in front of a machine somewhere to press out widgets. They spent a lot of time selling me on the opportunity, effusing about what a great employer CPL was, how important they were to 'the client' (who was never named), what great perks were on offer and how easy it was to get promoted. The interview itself came down to a handful of questions that I'll paraphrase here:

What is your understanding of the role? As far as I know, somebody using Facebook sees something they don't like and reports it, then it lands on my desk, and I have to apply some rules that your client will give me to decide what to do with it.

If you see something that you think is okay, but the rules tell you to delete it, or if you think it should be deleted but the rules say it's okay, what would you do? Just follow the rules. I assume Facebook have put a lot of thought into what they allow and what they don't, and you can't have thousands of people all doing whatever they like. So the job is to put your personal opinions aside and just implement the client's policies.

You might occasionally see content that some people may find disturbing. Are you okay with that? Well, I'm a mature adult with lots of life experience, and I'm pretty tough. I don't like horror movies, but I'm sure it'll be fine.

It's mostly a very boring, repetitive job: you'll be doing the same thing over and over. Does that bother you? I'm a teacher. I spend half my life grading homework. People give me something they've written, and I have to evaluate it against some standard, for hundreds of students. I imagine it's much the same. [Would you like me to kiss your butt while I'm here? I need this job.]

—

I'm beating myself up for being an idiot and taking this job, but was it my fault?

I definitely wouldn't have been sitting in that room if I had known what I was getting into. I sat there glibly claiming to be resilient and tough because I had never been traumatised by spending all day every day immersed in blood, vitriol, nastiness, hate and petty-minded spite. I didn't know what I was saying. How could I? Nobody at CPL made any effort to help me understand what the job was really like.

The recruiter interviewing me didn't help. She had probably never even been to the Facebook offices and had certainly never done the work. She went through the motions[†] as she got the answers she needed to fill her quota and make her bonus, just as I pretended to be a perfect fit for the job when the smart response would have been to run away screaming. We were all playing our parts in a theatre. I wasn't going to ask difficult questions, just as she wasn't going to volunteer difficult detail. Everyone just played the game and pretended everything was fine.

† I have concluded that the entire recruiting industry and HR profession is basically a parasite on the real business of delivering a product or service. Greg Jackson, an entrepreneur whose multi-billion pound company, Octopus Energy, employs 1,600 people, describes it as 'infantilising' employees and expects managers to hire and manage their own teams instead. So far it seems to be working for him.

I must have given them the right answers because the next day they sent me an email offering me a job as a Community Operations Analyst working for CPL Onsite Facebook, for the princely salary of €12.98 per hour, plus 25 per cent after 8 p.m.[†] They even offered me a few quid for a taxi home after midnight. I was in! My new life was beginning and I was delighted. What could go wrong?

† That same year, according to data shared with the Companies Registration Office, the average package (salary plus shares) paid to Facebook's regular staff, the ones not employed by CPL, was €154,000 per year.

TWO

STEPPING UP
AND LEANING IN

In May 2017 Mark Zuckerberg announced that Facebook was going to increase the number of people working on 'Community Operations' from 4,500 to 7,000 worldwide. (Almost all of them would be outsourced through companies like CPL.)

That announcement itself is an insight into the way Facebook thinks about content moderation. You can double your budget for an activity and ask your staff to work overtime, but you can't just hire ten new people to work in your restaurant if there are no experienced restaurant staff available. Did Zuckerberg think that you can hire just anybody and expect them to take responsibility for policing the internet and protecting the public with only a few weeks' training?

At this time, CPL employed around 400 people on-site at Facebook's European headquarters, mostly working on the Access and Authenticity side of T&S. Suddenly CPL needed another 400 people to do content moderation and to find desks for them in a building that was already quite crowded. These people needed to be trained, managed and supported, and the sense I got from CPL on my first day was that this was an organisation pulling out all the stops to do the impossible in response to an urgent crisis. The excitement was palpable as soon as I walked in to the airy lobby beneath the 'Move fast and break things' sign and joined the queue of eager, fresh-faced recruits at the security desk. I was asked for my name and an ID. A CPL manager standing to one side confirmed I was supposed to be there and I was given a temporary visitor badge on a yellow lanyard. A friendly Lithuanian guy in a blue security T-shirt showed me how to use it to get through the barrier, and a woman from Bolivia nervously waved me around the corner to the classroom where I would be spending the next week or two.

She didn't seem a hundred per cent sure of herself, and I think a lot of people were stepping into new roles, to fill the gaps as they appeared, gamely doing their best at jobs they may not have been prepared for or properly supported to do. It was exhilarating. There seemed to be opportunities everywhere to make yourself useful and get promoted.

They were maybe 40 or 50 of us newbies in the classroom, which was frankly a bit shabby and cramped due to the miscellaneous stuff stacked against the walls. It was one of the larger rooms in the building and seemed like it was usually used for storage but had been pressed into temporary service as a classroom while the organisation switched to high gear. Pretty much all of us were working on the principle that this job was our foot in the door at Facebook and nobody minded sitting on those cheap stackable plastic office chairs for a few days while we got started. We wanted to make our mark, advance, get hired by Facebook directly and build lucrative high-status careers with a brand that was still relatively untarnished at the time. It was also right next to the canteen so at least we didn't have far to go to get fed.

The food was pretty good too, and everything was completely free. It was perfectly acceptable to come into work early, get a full cooked breakfast and/or all the fruit you could eat from the servery, then eat a big lunch and treat yourself to dinner at the end of the day as well – or even take it home. There were maybe half a dozen options each day for the main course – which changed day by day and always catered for anyone with special dietary requirements – a huge table of various cakes and other desserts, a salad bar and fridges full of soft drinks, all there for the taking and dished out cheerfully by a hard-working and friendly kitchen team hailing mostly from Eastern Europe.

We were all impressed. The lunch queue moved quickly and there were lots of booths and seating areas with big stuffed couches to sit on while we ate. Even the Wi-Fi worked. It had the feel of a decent restaurant in the central courtyard of a tall building, bathed in natural light with the ceiling fifty feet above us. We sat there that first lunchtime, excitedly making new friends and talking about why we were there, bloated and basking in the shared anticipation of our futures. We had all seen the news reports highlighting the need for content moderation and the importance of the work. Most of us believed that we were there to make a difference and to build careers in this new industry. We wanted to be Batman, to save the world, or at least we wanted to save the innocents from the terrible things the world wanted to share with them. But first we had to get through the rest of the paperwork.

Onboarding was a bit of a rigmarole, especially for somebody like me who had always simply been hired by clients face to face. This was my first brush with HR departments and systemised hiring at scale. Simple things like proof of entitlement to work in Ireland and providing references were straightforward enough, but before we could start we also had to go through some kind of security vetting which was handled by a company called HireRight LLC.

HireRight sent me some forms to fill in giving permission for background checks and requiring a list of my previous addresses. I had a couple of addresses in Ireland, one in China, one in Turkey, two in Bulgaria and then ran out of space on the form before I could list all of the other places I had lived. However, it seemed like this was enough information for them, assuming they did anything with it, and on 19 June 2017, I found myself in that classroom in GC4, being asked to sign a contract with CPL that included some pretty frightening clauses.

The most obviously problematic was the NDA, the non-disclosure agreement, essentially a line in the contract saying that I wouldn't discuss the client's business with anyone. It mentioned that further details were available in the employee handbook but we weren't given a copy of it at the time. This handbook, together with the guidance given in training, really laid down the law and basically told us we were not to discuss anything with anybody, ever, not even our significant others. It was like taking a vow of silence.

This was justified at the time by reference to legitimate corporate secrets such as new products in development, which they illustrated with images of press reports about a 'Facebook phone' that someone had leaked. They also implied that there was a safety risk from hypothetical members of the public who might get angry about moderating decisions and target us. We were advised to hide our shiny new Facebook ID badges when travelling on the bus so as not to get into arguments with members of the public, and to not really answer if our friends and family asked us what we do for work. I quickly got into the habit of just telling people that I deleted dick pics for a living, which is a simple non-controversial answer and also quite a conversation-stopper.

We were permitted to list ourselves on LinkedIn with 'CPL Onsite Facebook' as our employer, not just Facebook, although I'm not sure if this was policed. There was also a line in the contract giving Facebook the right to collect data and monitor our private communications on their platform. Nobody highlighted this; it was just skimmed over during induction. If I had realised at the time what I was signing away, and how it could be used against people, I would have … I don't know what I would have done. I needed the job and drawing attention to myself by pointing out that this was illegal would probably have been a bad move. It was like telling us that we 'might occasionally see content that some people may find disturbing' during the interview. You accept it because it's presented very matter-of-factly, you don't have time to think about it, and you need the job so you just tell yourself it will be okay.

What would you do if you had started a new job and on the first day your employer insisted that you give them the password to your Facebook account so that they could read your personal communications, record your search history and friend requests, track your movements, your likes and dislikes, and so on? This is what we agreed to without realising it, except it wasn't our employer, CPL, doing the monitoring; it was our employer's client, Facebook.

We signed without a second thought. The starting point for access to all the internal systems is your personal Facebook account. Once you've logged in to that you can then log into Workplace – a kind of duplicate Facebook but only for staff – and all the other tools or resources you might need. It was all linked to our Facebook accounts so there was no way to separate your private life from your work. Around the time I started, *The Guardian* reported that several members of the anti-terrorism team based in Dublin had learned that some of their family members – many of whom were living in unstable Middle-Eastern countries – had received friend requests from people affiliated with ISIS. It transpired that due to some oversight by Facebook, the people running ISIS propaganda pages were able to discover who was deleting them and who their friends and family were.

Paperwork complete, we were issued with our company laptop computers. I got a shiny new high-end Lenovo, fully loaded with the latest Windows and all the software I could need. I thought about the mobile phone I had thrown away when I left China. It had seemed safest to just assume that it was riddled with state-sponsored spyware, and now here I was looking at a machine built by an arm of the Chinese government specifically for use by a major Western company that specialised in surveillance.

This thought was replaced by another when I saw the guy next to me excitedly playing with his computer.

'Is that an Apple?' I asked innocently.

'Yeah,' he replied. 'I wonder how they knew which I preferred. You normally use Windows?'

I nodded, and we discussed how Facebook knew what kind of computer everyone preferred without even asking. It's pretty easy to do because every time you use their service your device sends all kinds of information to them. Every device you use, your location, everything you type, every photo you upload, everything you look at, how long you look at it for and how fast you scroll down your newsfeed – it's all collected and analysed in case it ever comes in useful. Most of us know this at some level but being shown targeted ads somehow feels different from being handed a tool by someone who has decided for you what you want. Move fast with stable infrastructure, indeed.

I put these thoughts out of my head because it was time for training to begin, and I was immediately struck by two things. The first was that most of the people in the training did not speak English as their first language. The Dublin moderation effort serves many different markets around the world and employs people from a huge diversity of backgrounds and cultures. However, the training material seemed to be written on the assumption that everybody was a native speaker of English with legal training and immersed in Western (i.e. Silicon Valley) culture.

The second thing was that there was no course design as such. The trainers plunged into a series of intensive lectures about policy and rules that didn't seem to be connected or have an overarching theme. It was all theoretical and academic, and the first week of training was characterised by us spending our downtime hanging out in the canteen, trying to make sense of it all. People clustered together with others who spoke the same language as them, trying to help each other decipher it, all of us fighting a rising dread that we were expected to remember all of this stuff.

At the start of the second week of training, one of the site management team came to the classroom with a worried look on her face. Thankfully, someone had noticed that things weren't going very well. The problem was quite a simple one and easily rectified once it was recognised and understood.

New hires would normally be embedded with the team they were to join and assigned a buddy – someone that they would follow and observe as they did the work whenever they were not in formal training. Our training schedule even had buddy time built into it – but we had no buddies.

Due to the shortage of space, we were going to be working an evening shift and hot-desking with the daytime guys. We were the first batch of recruits for the evening shift, so there were no established teams for us to join. When we weren't in the classroom we were just hanging around at a loose end with nowhere to go. We had never observed anyone doing the work, so we didn't know how the work was done.

The process is as follows: a moderator is presented with a piece of content to review, judges it based on a set of rules called the Implementation Standards (IS) and then clicks through a menu of options to identify the rule they're implementing. So, if you see a pair of bare breasts,[†] you click on 'delete', then 'adult nudity' (the relevant policy), then 'female breasts' (the relevant sub-section of the policy). It's very simple some of the time, but if the comment says, 'I'm going to kill that Fenian', then you may have to look at the various policies on hate speech, credible violence and bullying to determine which (if

† Female breasts, of course. Men are allowed to show their nipples whenever they like; women may only do so in the context of medical information or political protest, so there is a companion document called the Known Questions (KQs), which goes into excruciating detail about when a breast is considered to be bare and how to identify a political protest.

any) action to take. As a result, you keep the IS open on your computer so that you can refer back to it as you're working.

The training we were having was supposed to help us understand the detail of the IS. However, we didn't know that it even existed. Every day we were given lectures about different specific policies, but we didn't know what to do with them. We didn't know about the menu of options. The training was all just theoretical discussions about whether 'Fenian' was a pejorative term, a slur, a slang term denoting a specific combination of protected characteristics, and so on. Without understanding the big picture, it seemed like a mass of unconnected information and we thought we had to memorise it all.

All it took was for someone to give us a 15-minute demonstration of how the work was done, and everything changed. As soon as we understood, the dread was replaced with relief and everyone relaxed – except for yours truly. I had 15 years of adult education experience and sat at the back muttering about how to design a course properly, grumbling that nobody knew how to do their jobs. Unfortunately, I did it quietly enough to not draw attention to myself and get fired, so I wasn't spared the nightmare that was to come.

Some of our trainers had never stood at the front of a classroom before, didn't know anything about training and were not familiar with the training material. I felt quite sorry for them. Before I started the job I was excited to see what innovative techniques Facebook would bring to the training. I was expecting immense resources and expertise assigned to maximise the efficiency and effectiveness of teaching us to do this vital work.

Instead, I got a non-native English speaker struggling through grammatically complex sentences and occasionally admitting they didn't know what some of the words meant in front of a room full of stressed new recruits who were also challenged by the complex language and didn't know what was going on or what was required of them.

This is not the fault of any of the trainers. To the best of my knowledge they were paid an extra 50 cents per hour, were given very little training or support and in some cases had reluctantly volunteered to do a job that needed to be done but that they didn't feel qualified for. They were doing their best in difficult circumstances and, after a couple of days of this, I realised that they also had absolutely no freedom in what they did. Their job was to stand at the front of the room and read PowerPoint slides aloud. They weren't allowed to deviate from the script and they weren't given any time or freedom to improvise or improve on what was there. There was an implicit assumption that Facebook as an entity had already provided everything that could be required and that the trainers were not adding any value.

The problem is a phenomenon I call 'Death Star by PowerPoint', and it's so common in the corporate world (and sadly in real classrooms too) that most people take it for granted. Back in 1977, there was a movie called *Star Wars*. Do yourself a favour: take a quick look on YouTube and find the scene where a group of pilots are being briefed for their attack on the Death Star. For me as a teacher, it's a beautiful scene because of the way the presentation is handled. The person giving the talk is the expert and is exercising leadership as well as sharing information. He is in charge of the room, the centre of attention, and as he talks there are images and animations on the screen behind him which illustrate what he is saying and make everything clear.

The great thing about having control over your visuals is that you can adapt to the needs of your audience, which is the essence of leadership. Interaction with the people you are teaching, feedback from them and your awareness of how well your message is being received all enable you to change what you do in response to their needs and be better at your job.

Good education requires the learners to be engaged with the endeavour and the person in charge to be focused on the audience. Questions and opinions are welcomed. In the Star Wars briefing scene, we see the pilots engaging with the task in front of them and discussing it actively. It's a great example of how a classroom should be managed because everyone leaves the room knowing exactly what they have to do and they're eager to go do it. Now imagine the animated graphic behind the person in charge has been replaced with a PowerPoint slide describing the Death Star in words. With bullet points. Everything has changed. The lesson is on the screen, not being given by the expert at the front of the room. The audience is focused on reading the words on the screen, instead of listening to the expert. The expert is no longer focused on his audience. They have to turn away from them to read the words on the screen out loud, which is a pointless activity because everybody is already reading at their own speed.

Forcing someone to stand at the front of the room and read your words from a slide is not only disrespectful to your audience but also sends a message that the trainer doesn't know anything either (even if they actually do). It undermines everyone's faith in the process and it's a terrible way to teach anyone anything. I expected better from one of the world's great companies, especially one that has invested so much money and effort into finding new and innovative ways to put information in front of people. I guess we weren't worth it for them.

After a few more days of this, we were finally let loose to do the work. We had been in training during normal office hours, 9.00 a.m. to 5.30 p.m., but on the Thursday – day nine of training – we came in at 5.30 p.m. instead to start the first evening shift and work with real content at last.

I have a lot of sympathy for the daytime staff who were being forced to give up their workspaces. They mostly tried to be nice, but there was some inevitable hostility from people who resented the changes that had to be made to accommodate us. Whereas before they had family photos, plants, gay pride flags, dinosaurs and other decorations on their desks, they had now been ordered to remove all personal items because they would be hot-desking with us. Instead of staying a bit late if they felt like it, to send a few emails or whatever, or simply leaving at their own pace as they chatted with colleagues, they were now faced with eager newbies hovering for them to give up their seats and get out of the way.

There were keyboards and large monitors on the desks, which we plugged our shiny new laptops into, but within days we started to arrive and find that cables were missing or the monitors had been unplugged – little acts of sabotage from people that were supposed to be on the same team as us. It was all very petty and these avoidable obstructive behaviours signified a lack of leadership that was to become increasingly apparent in the months that followed. Still, it wasn't a universal problem and the hostility gradually evaporated as everyone adapted.

Later on, we would be organised into teams according to geographic markets – UK and Ireland, Germany and Austria, France, Lithuania, Myanmar and so on – but at first we were just a mass of newbies. There were also a few regular staff who had volunteered to move from the day shift to the evening shift, usually in the hope that this would be a path to promotion, so there were a few experienced moderators around if we needed them. We were managed by a rotating cast of TLs (team leaders), on secondment from the day shift, usually there for just a week at a time.

There we all were, newly minted superheroes ready to save the world, being walked through the process of how to do the work. Nowadays Facebook relies on artificial intelligence (AI) to catch problem content before anyone even sees it, although a lot of it is still reviewed by humans after being flagged. However, back then it was up to the public to report things they didn't like. Everything we reviewed had been reported by someone who didn't like it and then put into a queue depending on what they found so objectionable. There were queues for child abuse, queues for hate speech and terrorism, and queues for pornography. Most of these queues were also separated into individual 'markets' as well, which is what Facebook calls language groups and countries. There was a French spam queue, a German spam queue, a Norwegian one and so on.

Then there was the Global Photo Pornography queue. This was just images from all over the world, sometimes accompanied by text, which needed to be reviewed because they included some measure of nudity or sexual content. The queue was usually worked by a team in India managed by Accenture, but apparently they were getting overwhelmed by the sheer volume of smut on Facebook. For the first month or so, this was where we played.

Since there weren't enough of us to form market teams mirroring the day shift, they put us into a holding pattern on this queue while they continued to recruit and train more people. We were doing something useful but not let loose on the real work until we had a bit of experience and proper management.

I don't remember the first actual ticket that I reviewed but I'm pretty sure it was benign enough – probably a young woman in a bikini, an exotic dancer or even something more pornographic. In any event, it didn't bother me. For some reason, it was mostly naked women, with far fewer naked men. However, now and then somebody would see something more extreme and call out excitedly to the people around them to come and see.

A few particular examples come to mind. In one case a naked masked man has his hands tied behind his back and is facing a woman in high heels and lingerie. The scene is viewed from the side so both figures are visible and you can *feel* the power the woman puts into it when she kicks the man in the balls. He staggers a bit but stays standing. She does it again. And again. And again. I don't remember how many times she kicked him, but my eyes were watering and I remember the discussions and the frantic references to the IS as we tried to figure out what to do with it. If somebody is being physically hurt and they are restrained, that's torture. But what if it's voluntary, as this appeared to be? How can you tell whether it's voluntary? We looked at the various definitions of sexual activity, the rules for what is and isn't considered nudity and what body parts must be visible to activate different policies.

You're probably wondering why this was so difficult. It's because there is a hierarchy of actions. Some policies are more important than others, although they're not listed in order of importance in the IS, so it's not enough just to delete something for the first violation you become aware of. You have to consider all the rules that may be applicable and delete the content for the right reason. If you take the right action for the wrong reason, that's counted as a mistake. Delete the naked woman for being naked and miss the fact that she's trying to sell you fake LV-branded goods, and that means you've failed to implement the most important policy, which was the prohibition on spam content.

Another time, somebody near to me stepped back from the desk with a sharp intake of breath. I looked over to see a bored-looking man having sex with a very relaxed-looking golden retriever. At least that one was straightforward! Every time you make a decision you press a key combination to tell the system which policy you're invoking. As soon as you press the final key the decision is logged and the next ticket is loaded. It's just a relentless bombardment of image after image and you never know what's up next.

One day I was blasting through the queue, seeing a ticket every few seconds because I had mastered the relevant key combinations for the narrow range of violations that we were seeing, when suddenly my screen was filled with a close-up video of a man masturbating. I mean really close. It was a big monitor and it was completely filled with the man's hand and genitals. I did the standard scream of comic disgust to signify to my colleagues that something interesting was happening and in no time there were half a dozen of us looking on in awe and horror.

It was obvious that the content had to be deleted and which of the policies were being violated. It was a no-brainer really, but I announced quite loudly that I didn't want to touch the computer and asked for someone else to do it. The people around me all shied away, expressing some variant of 'I'm not going near that'. After a pause, one of the girls leaned in, pressed the key combo to delete the content and then picked up the wet wipes that were on every desk for cleaning between shifts. She wiped down the keyboard, then the whole desk and finally her own hands, before going back to her workstation.

I don't think we realised it at the time, but we felt 'touched' by what we were seeing, and usually we didn't have the time to properly process it.

Although everything we saw had been reported as pornography, it wasn't just pornography that we were seeing. They were often other issues and the most memorable of them was the first time any of us saw suicide or self-harm content.

Somebody a few desks away suddenly blurted out that they had a suicide and didn't know what to do. We all came running, of course, consumed by an eager dread. We had all sat through the lecture but this was the first time any of us had had to deal with the situation for real and it was terrifying. The person in the video – it may have been a live stream – was cutting their arms and there were indications that they planned to kill themselves. All that any of us could think was 'Fuck, fuck, what do I do?'

The IS contain detailed descriptions of what is and isn't to be considered imminent harm. This is treated differently from promotion, encouragement or depiction of suicide, which is in turn different from talking about suicide. They're all different and require different responses from the moderators, so it's all very granular and precisely defined. We were frantically trying to find and apply the relevant rules to know which specific action to take and then trying to figure out how to do it. I remember the guy who was assigned the ticket was really stressed and said several times that he didn't know what to do.

One of the duty TLs showed up and shooed us all away while he walked my colleague through the steps he had to take. I went back to my desk and looked up the rules around imminent harm and which content should be escalated to the safety team. Then I looked for the document explaining how to escalate something to the safety team, which took a while to find. You have to send an email in a specific format, so I made an email template listing all the relevant information required and the address to send it to. I then stored it in my mail program so I would be able to respond quickly, and have the right resources in place, when it happened to me. I knew it would happen to me eventually. It's an inevitable part of the job, something we were realising we would all face at some point, and I wanted to be prepared.

I couldn't help putting on my teacher hat at this point and advising all my colleagues to do the same. I think this should have been done during training. If you're expecting somebody to deal with an urgent life-or-death situation, isn't it a good idea to have them prepare themselves mentally by putting the resources in place that they will need? All trades and professions have their toolkits and preparing your toolkit is part of becoming an expert, making yourself ready to do your job. This training failure caused a great deal of unnecessary stress for several people and I can still recall it vividly five years later. I look back and wonder whether anyone was really in charge, whether anyone had a handle on what was going on and what needed to be done to keep things running smoothly and safely. I can see now how close an emotional connection we felt to some of the things we saw, and how much avoidable stress was being created by the lack of leadership.

—

In fairness, experiences like these were very much the exception at the time. Global Photo Pornography was a fairly benign queue and we quickly started to find the work very easy and repetitive. On a typical evening, I would work around 1,200 tickets, a new image every 15–20 seconds, without pushing myself too hard. At this point, our supervision was minimal as well. There was something of a party atmosphere most of the time and a fair amount of goofing and joking around. We also had access to Workplace, the special Facebook site for staff with 'tribes' (Facebook Groups) for different teams. Pretty soon we started to see posts appearing in the evening shift tribe saying things like 'Party at my place after work, free beer' or 'Will somebody please show me how to lock my computer when I leave my desk?'

These were 'frapes', practical jokes played on people who had left their computers unattended. I didn't think it was a particularly funny thing to do after the first few times I saw it but didn't take much notice of it until it nearly happened to me. Somebody sitting nearby had asked my opinion on something, and I had taken a few steps away from my desk to take a look. When I turned back around, another newbie, 'James', was standing at my desk typing on my computer. I nudged the guy next to me, crept up behind James, seized him theatrically and whispered 'gotcha' or something similar.

It was a harmless enough encounter and I wasn't going to make anything of it until he told me that he was on a mission to encourage people to lock their computers when unattended and had been detailed to do it by Zandra, one of the TLs on duty.

I was quite shocked by this. It's very easy for someone to copy behaviour that they've seen online without really thinking about it, but it's quite another for someone in authority to instruct them to do it. I pointed out to him that he was accessing a secure network using somebody else's credentials. Even though no harm was intended and no harm was done, one of our first orientation lectures stressed the importance of security, user privacy, integrity etc. I was pretty sure that this kind of fraping was probably a fireable offence if the client ever became aware of it, and it didn't seem right that a TL didn't understand this.

I had a look in the company handbook, and my suspicions were confirmed: accessing the secure internal network with someone else's credentials, for any reason whatsoever, was explicitly forbidden and was grounds for instant dismissal. Good intentions, and whether you do any harm, were not relevant. The rule was to never do it under any circumstances and sending someone else to do it was putting them in jeopardy.

I am someone who is used to identifying and fixing mistakes and I don't have the employee mindset of keeping your head down that was essential in a company like this, so I dashed off a quick informal message telling Zandra what had happened and that I believed it could have bad consequences if people kept on doing it. I naively thought I was just doing her a favour, giving her a heads-up about something she maybe hadn't thought through.

You can guess how that turned out. A few minutes later I was pulled from my desk and taken into a meeting room where a very defensive TL told me that it was just a joke, it happened all the time and there was no need for me to start quoting the staff handbook at anyone.

I apologised and we left the room. I went back to my desk, grinned at the people around me who were having a good laugh at my stupid expense and forgot all about it. Eventually. I was quite bemused by the episode for a while, but the work displaces everything else from your brain, so it was gone from my mind by the end of the shift. (But it wasn't gone for good. A few months later, as we will see in Chapter 8, I got involved in the nitty-gritty of Facebook's internal privacy and security policies to try and help a colleague keep their job. If you make a name for yourself as someone who will point out wrongdoing, sooner or later people come to you for help and advice and then everything goes to shit.)

Just after this little drama, I was talking to a more senior manager one day and mentioned that I wasn't learning anything from the Global Photo Pornography queue any longer. I was keen, I wanted to move up, we were just in a holding pattern and I was sure there must be useful work that needed to be done, so I stupidly asked if there was any other more important work she could give me.

There's a saying that you should be careful what you wish for because you might get it, and I certainly got my wish that day. She asked me if I knew any other languages and the next thing I knew I was visited at my desk by the TL of the German daytime team to set me up with access to the German hate speech queue. Be careful what you wish for, indeed!

—

The next week or so was incredibly challenging and exhilarating. My productivity dropped from maybe 1,200 tickets per night to a maximum of 250 as I struggled to interpret a whole new world of crazy in a language that I didn't really speak that well and to apply complex rules I had only just been introduced to. I was tremendously pleased to be given the work, I felt like this was something that mattered and it was fascinating to begin to see and understand a problem that was just starting to be recognised by the wider world. I felt like I was at the cutting edge in the next battleground of ideas, although most of the time I didn't know what I was doing.

If you see a photo of graffiti in a children's play park, written in the style of the German Empire, calling for strength and national unity, what the hell does that even mean? The German Empire was dissolved in 1919, before the rise of the Nazis, but the imagery and traditions of that empire have been claimed by the extreme right. What would you do with a message like that? What should the rules say?

This was my introduction to the world of online hate, misinformation, confusion and complex nuanced messages written by people who probably weren't even clear themselves about what their intentions were. I was stressed as hell (and isolated from the team I was supporting because we worked at different times of the day) but I loved it. The work was demanding and important and I felt that I was doing something meaningful. The people around me, still immersed in naked women, were quite envious of me as I luxuriated in the responsibility and importance of my new role.

There was some issue at the time with the air conditioning and it seemed to be always either too warm or too cold, so I started bringing a light blanket to work. The desks could be raised and lowered at will, and I used to stand at my desk with my blanket draped over my shoulders, listening to 1980s synth-pop music on big noise-cancelling headphones that tech support handed out on request, more or less dancing as I navigated the intricacies of the German far right. I must have looked like a right idiot, but I was happy.

Weirdly – something I mentioned when I started talking to journalists a long time later – when we started the job we thought we were superheroes, there to save the world. I wasn't consciously thinking of those evenings dressed like a kid playing at being Batman as I patrolled the mean streets of the internet, but I did learn something interesting from a researcher who had studied Arvato, the German counterpart to CPL that runs the moderation effort in Berlin. They use the superhero metaphor in their recruiting ads! Their pitch is all about fighting the good fight and protecting the innocent. Moderators are portrayed as superheroes without whom civilisation would fall. Maybe I was infected with this idea virus by the German TL when she came to see me?

I started the job at the beginning of June, and by mid-August there were hundreds of people on the evening shift. At that point we started to get additional training for what was being called graph integrity (GI), later referred to as 'access and authenticity'.

It was interesting to me that I would ask my colleagues, including the people training us, what GI meant and they would just shrug their shoulders. This kind of apathy was a shock for me. It's possibly something that recruiters look for when they hire people for this kind of role and maybe it's my curiosity that was my undoing at Facebook. There seemed to be a culture of acceptance, compliance and institutionalised thoughtlessness. Asking questions and having opinions just got me into trouble.

Anyway, my best guess is that the name was a reference to the 'social graph', a buzzword from 2007 or so that referred to the famous diagram of the connections between all Facebook users. Maintaining the integrity of the social graph meant ensuring that everybody on the platform was an authentic user with only one profile and abiding by the rules governing their profile.

GI work was all about investigating reports of inauthentic profiles and helping genuine users who were locked out of their accounts for some reason. These were very straightforward problems to solve and had been CPL's bread and butter for many years. This was the work that my wife mostly did, and that of my friend Maria, whose story I tell in Chapter 8. It was exceedingly tedious work with very little thinking or analysis involved most of the time. You just opened the ticket and worked through the flowchart provided for that specific queue.

For some reason, however, most of the people I did this training with agreed with me that they still felt they didn't know what they were doing. The people teaching us the procedures were so familiar with them and had internalised so much that was not written down that they were making jumps we couldn't follow. We did sometimes try asking a lot of questions in the training, but time was limited and the trainers were supposed to just follow the lesson plan they had been given. Anything we didn't understand immediately 'would make sense once we started to do the work'. This was the case 95 per cent of the time, but then when we encountered something that wasn't covered by the training or reference material, we would find ourselves staring at the screen, flummoxed.

I did GI work for only a month and regularly found myself pinging TLs or other experts for guidance. Even though it eventually became a very small part of my workload, by the end of September I had made a total of three formal requests for follow-up training for myself and my group.

Newbies were given a two-month ramp-up period during which their quality and productivity were hardly monitored. I've heard Facebook executives in interviews talking about the ratio of formal to informal training, the latter being considered the main part. Training newbies is basically everyone's responsibility and the formal rules and procedures are there for reference only. This is kind of odd, considering the way quality control is done, but we'll talk about that later. For now, let's just focus on getting our heads around the working environment in the first few months.

The bulk of my GI work was centred around preventing Nigerian scammers – known as Yahoo! boys – from creating fake accounts that they could use for various nefarious purposes. This was a huge problem and continues to be so today. I would see hundreds of new accounts being created every day by people who claimed to be in the UK but whose IP address showed them to be in Nigeria. This discrepancy alone caused the account creation to be paused, an automated request for ID documents to be sent and everything referred to a human operator for review.

There were various warning signs which would immediately cause us to keep it on hold. Our job was to verify the identity documents they would send – and what a weird and wonderful bunch they were! Many were obviously fake, but sometimes they would obtain a copy of a genuine document from somewhere and try to create an account in the same name, using the documents over and over. If we had a good reason we would request that they send a photo of themselves holding the ID next to their face. The most common reasons were that it was obviously fake or simply that we had already seen that same ID so many times that we recognised it when we saw it.

I still remember some of the names the scammers used. One of the most prolific offenders was a hunky blond chap named Thor Odinson, who looked like a Norse god or a movie star and used to send copies of his driver's license to us almost every day as he tried again and again to create new accounts. Another woman, who admittedly looked more plausibly Nigerian, was the singer Whitney Houston. Despite being dead, she would send a copy of her passport several times a week, as did one Michelle Obama. Admittedly Michelle wasn't as persistent – I guess she had a lot of other things to do and Facebook scams were just a side hustle for her.

It amazed me that there was no facility for us to label an ID as fake or stolen so that automated systems could detect and deal with them without us having to spend our time on them. It's possible that privacy and data protection laws make this impossible. I do know that identity documents sent to Facebook were only stored for a short period while the case was resolved and then deleted from the system. I guess there are legal implications for Facebook if they start saving copies of identity documents, even if they believe them to be fake, and this illustrates how the world is still struggling to deal with issues of privacy and trust in the online realm. Should big tech be allowed to store a copy of Michelle Obama's passport, or yours or mine, for any reason? Even straightforward issues get very complicated very fast when you start thinking about them in any detail.[†]

—

My first few months in the job were a fascinating insight into how hard it is to get things right and to get things right all the time, on a massive scale. Aside from the simple fact that there is no global consensus about what is acceptable and what isn't, writing clear definitions to set your boundaries and ensuring that tens of thousands of people reviewing millions of pieces of content every day all make the correct decisions all the time on complex nuanced issues is an enormous challenge.

[†] Apple have a similar problem with certain people collecting sexually explicit images of children on their phones and then storing copies on the iCloud. Their solution to this is to compare every image to a database of known child porn as it is uploaded. Whenever they get a match it is referred to a human moderator to make a decision on. This means that someone somewhere has to spend all day looking at photos of children being abused.

THREE

IT'S NOT PERSONAL, IT'S JUST BUSINESS

By September 2017, after three months in the job, I more or less felt I understood what was going on, and since then I've gained the benefit of several years' hindsight and insider information. This may be a good moment to pause the story and clarify a few details, starting with who I was actually working for.

My legal employer was CPL and everyone I ever dealt with was also a CPL employee. There was a whole management structure above me, and then alongside that there was also 'the client', Facebook. We were 'on-site' and worked in a Facebook building using computers provided by Facebook, connected to Facebook's internal network, and did work assigned by Facebook according to processes laid down by Facebook.

Some of the people a step or two above me in the food chain liaised with, or reported to, Facebook full-time employees (FTEs), who referred to us as contractors, but they also had CPL managers who in turn were also accountable to people at Facebook as well as their CPL bosses. I learned later that Facebook was monitoring our communications and performance and occasionally exercised the power to terminate the work placement of CPL employees, so it was never really clear which company was responsible for us, our work or indeed anything.

Even though the basic premise of this book, and my own experiences with Facebook, might suggest that I'm hostile to the company, that's a long way from the truth. My gripes are related to specific fixable issues only rather than a generalised hatred of what they do for a living.

If you're reading this you're probably a Facebook user and there's a good chance you have accounts with other social media companies and websites with moderation policies as well. These are useful services. People stick with them for the benefits they provide and I can see the value in them. Facebook is hardly unique in struggling with content moderation. I was deeply entangled in that topic years before I was even aware that Facebook existed.

I lived for a long time in Taiwan and worked as a freelance English teacher, part of a large community of foreigners who had been drawn to the island by the promise of easy money and a good life as an expert in speaking my own language. In 2002 I was an eager newbie who didn't know anything about teaching English or the local culture. My most valuable resource was a chat website called forumosa.com. This was a community site run by volunteers on which I could ask questions and get the answers I needed, so long as I could navigate the snarkiness and banter that some of the community's members excelled at. As I stayed longer in Taiwan and turned into an old hand I eventually became one of those volunteers and started helping to moderate the discussion forums, to keep things civil and friendly to newbies with questions.

We had to develop our own rules and systems, and as a starting point, we needed clarity about what we were trying to achieve. I think it's important to share a key principle here: the key metric for any online service is user engagement – how many people are visiting and how long are they staying? – and content moderation is basically the job of managing a community so that the maximum number of people can participate in safety and feel welcome. If your business relies on showing ads to users to make money, engagement is the most important thing. It's as simple as that.

In moderation, if you are too quick to jump on people for every transgression, that has a chilling effect on the community that you're trying to build and people stop visiting. However, taking a hands-off approach, and letting anybody say anything they liked, allows the loudest, most aggressive voices to dominate the conversations and turns everyone else off. This also harms the community you're trying to build.

If I were running Facebook I would study content moderation as a business process and optimise it to get the maximum return on investment. I would want to know how much content moderation is too much and how much is too little. I would plot a graph showing expenditure on content moderation on one axis and user engagement on the other.

Somewhere on that graph, I would put a big red X identifying the sweet spot where profits are maximised. Wouldn't you do that if you were running that business?

There's a lot of debate about how much content moderation is appropriate, and one day at Facebook I had a conversation with a colleague that later came back to bite him in the arse. We were leaving a policy update meeting in which there had been some discussion about the interpretation of content that some of us believed should be taken down.

The ruling from further up the food chain was to leave it alone, and my colleague was a little bit frustrated. I stupidly said to him in private that Facebook didn't care about right or wrong, only user engagement. I told him that controversial content gets more user engagement because people talk about it and repost it and Facebook gets to put more advertising alongside it and make more money. I remember he stared at me with a slightly shocked expression on his face and didn't reply.

Some months later, just after I had left the job, an undercover reporter from Dispatches (the investigative Channel 4 programme) joined my old team and worked briefly as a content moderator, while also filming everything using a hidden camera built into his clothing. At some point during his time there, my unfortunate colleague repeated my off-the-cuff remark to him and it was subsequently broadcast on national TV.

Channel 4 portrayed this as being official Facebook policy and implied that all moderators had been instructed to permit outrageous and divisive comments that the general public would disapprove of, to make more money, forcing senior executives from Facebook to give interviews denying this.

Although my colleague's face was blurred he remained readily identifiable to anyone who knew him – so I owe him an apology! Mate, if you're reading this, you know who you are, and I am sorry. It was an uninformed opinion, not official company policy.

On the other hand, if we can't trust content moderators to think critically about every wild unsubstantiated claim they come across, what do we hire them for? I've researched the question in a bit more detail, and the evidence suggests that extreme viral content accounts for only a tiny percentage of what most people are looking at on Facebook. Getting rid of it probably doesn't hurt the bottom line, but it's interesting how many people nowadays are eager to believe this sort of outrageous claim made by people who are not paid for their expertise.

Any 'pure' calculation about content moderation, whether profit-driven or motivated by a desire to do good in society, is inevitably distorted by external pressures from what I call the 'outrage industry'.

For example, in the 1980s, when I was still in secondary school, home entertainment was revolutionised by the VHS video machine. We had three TV channels but suddenly instead of being able to watch only what these channels wanted to show us, and only at a time that suited them, we could go to a video shop and rent pretty much any movie. We thought it was great but there was no end to news stories written at the time about how unlimited access to violent movies was going to somehow create a generation of thugs and murderers that would terrorise polite society.

It never came to pass as predicted, just as the birth control pill and cannabis didn't lead to the collapse of civilisation in preceding decades. Later it was video games that the public had to be protected from and there have been plenty more examples of moral panics since then – situations in which a narrative has emerged about new ideas or technologies endangering people and society, without any real evidence to back them up.

These kinds of panic are often driven by people who have not only a limited understanding of whatever they are talking about but also an agenda of their own. There may be political or ideological reasons for their outrage, but often the outrage itself is what really matters to them. Provoking negative emotion is a great way to attract attention, boost a career, sell newspapers or attract eyeballs to look at screens. Academics need grants, politicians need votes and influencers need advertising revenue: what better way to get them than to point at something controversial and tell them it's dangerous?

We see this happening all the time on social media. That's part of the reason we have content moderation. CMs (content moderators) fight harmful narratives about immigration, climate change and what you 'should' be doing if you're a real man or a real patriot. At the same time, barely a day goes by without another high-profile story about harmful content or how the pressure to always present the best version of yourself leads to depression, vulnerability and so on. We hear all the time how social media is designed to be addictive and to manipulate and exploit users and how our always-on society is deeply unhealthy. It all comes from participants in the outrage industry, who have a vested interest in promoting a narrative of doom. Ironically, the online services most of us use every day are routinely demonised on those very same services by people who are doing exactly what they accuse others of doing.

Yes, there are risks and harms associated with using social media, but it seems pretty clear that most people have weighed the pros and cons and decided that the benefits outweigh the harms. Social media is here to stay: it's part of our culture now, an unstoppable force, and that makes it a very attractive target for the kind of people who like to get outraged about change. Without anyone to silence them, these voices are profiting by promoting the perception that extreme content is out of control and needs to be reined in. This adds to the pressure on social media companies to be seen to do something.

I don't think the big tech companies have done too bad a job of content moderation, but serious strategic mistakes have been made and they'll be discussed in the coming chapters. To understand the root causes of the issues I started to come up against, it's helpful to imagine the early days of Facebook: a handful of geeky students focused on building something until they get an email from someone who has forgotten their password. Someone has to be taken off task to deal with that every time it happens. As the project grows into a company, this kind of job is handed off to interns, but the scale continues to increase until some enterprising staffing agency calls up and offers to handle all the back office stuff so the team can focus on what they're good at.

This simple customer service function is outsourced to a company which also runs call centres for other brands. Later you start to see fake accounts being created, so you write some guidelines for your contractors to deal with that problem too and suddenly they are responsible for GI as well. It's a straightforward activity and easy to do quality control, so you agree on a standard – in this case insisting the workers make the right decision at least 98 per cent of the time – and leave them to it. You might have somebody on your team doing oversight, but you basically don't want to know anything about it. It's not part of your core business, even as your business grows, the volume of users increases and you're opening offices around the world for your core teams.

Then you start to get complaints about some of the things that some of your users are posting on your website. The outrage industry cranks up the rhetoric, and you worry that it might impact user engagement. You might even have an emotional 'I don't want that on my site' response of your own as well but it's a problem with user behaviour, like GI, so GI and content moderation both come under a new umbrella, trust and safety, and the T&S industry is born.

Facebook needs to figure out how to moderate posts from all over the world and make consistent decisions on a scale that has never been attempted before. Your team draws up a list of things they won't allow and hands it over to the outsource teams who are already taking care of GI. You detail some junior programmers to create some kind of technical system that allows them to review anything that gets reported and leave them to it again. By this time there are outsource teams all over the world, some of them embedded on-site with the core employees and some of them in sweatshops in the developing world. It probably makes perfect sense to hold them to the same 98 per cent quality standard as before and nobody thinks about it.

Then, as new behaviours emerge and your understanding of them increases, the complexity grows exponentially. I met CPL people who had been on-site at Facebook in Dublin since the early days, and they told me that when they started there were only two options to choose from when actioning a post: delete or ignore. By the time I arrived there were about 100 options to choose from because the list of unacceptable content had not only grown but also been subdivided into categories and subcategories, in a process that I call 'policy creep'.

Instead of simply deleting a piece of content, we had to say why. Delete>> category nudity>> subcategory penises>> subcategory erect penises. Or delete>> category spam>> subcategory restricted commercial activity>> subcategory fake branded goods. Then we needed a list of protected brands and branded goods to refer to and detailed descriptions explaining how much of a penis must be visible before it counts as visible. If it's 99 per cent obscured, or painted with latex, or it's a clearly defined outline beneath near see-through clothing does that count? How see-through does it have to be? What's the definition of see-through? And so on. The rules get ever more complex and detailed, the definitions ever more arcane.

This all comes from Menlo Park where Facebook has its headquarters in San Francisco (known internally as 'MPK'). Somebody with a salary of several hundred thousand dollars a year is being paid to create PowerPoint presentations explaining how to tell when a breast is being squeezed as part of a team of highly paid experts whose job it is to have conversations that seem ridiculous to the average person.

I am told that CMs these days now have not 100 but approximately 250 options to choose from when reviewing a piece of content. The cognitive load is immense. They have to hold all of these rules and definitions in their heads and be aware of all the clarifications and discussions about the rules in order to always choose the right one. The required quality score is still 98 per cent.

They are managed, trained and paid as if they are call centre workers dealing with simple administrative tasks, but the work they do is harder than that of most legal professionals. They're making hundreds of complex decisions every day under constant pressure to make their numbers, in a system that has grown up ad hoc in response to events rather than having been designed for purpose, and there are tens of thousands of them.

Facebook has given various estimates of the number of people doing T&S work around the world, and as of 2022, it appears to be around 40,000. All of these people need to be trained, managed, provided with a computer and a desk in an office, insured and paid an admittedly contemptuous salary. No matter how many corners you cut, this is an expensive operation. Facebook does describe it occasionally as an investment, but they're never very clear about what they expect to get in return. They never discuss the business case for moderation; it's always couched in terms of social obligation or public safety.

Which brings me to the next question, one I started asking myself after a few months on the job: who the hell writes this stuff?

I've been invited to all sorts of events since I've been talking about content moderation in public. I've managed to build something of a reputation as an informed and generally useful contributor to conversations about the practises and problems of the industry, and I've been privileged to talk to quite a few people who are or have been in fairly senior T&S positions. Most of them seem to be well-meaning and competent people, but I can't help reflecting that the T&S field attracts a particular kind of person with a particular educational and social background and that they share a fairly homogeneous set of beliefs and assumptions.

These people have a way of doing things, and a way of communicating, which they believe is best, and other kinds of people don't seem to be represented in their ranks. So how do they decide how other kinds of people should be allowed to behave?

Imagine a 'nice' academic like this trying to write a set of rules for moderating conversations in which people use the N-word. The users may be referring to themselves and their friends or a subset of the population they are hostile and contemptuous towards or using it naively because they've seen other people use it and think it's okay. It may be a term of endearment or an insult or occur in a discussion about when it's okay to use it (maybe as part of an academic enquiry or maybe in faux-innocence, as in 'But I call them that because ... '). Try writing the rules without discriminating against the people who think it describes them and without leaving the door open to online bullying or hate speech in other circumstances, bearing in mind that these users rarely have much appreciation for grammar either. It's no easy task, and if those styles of communication are alien to you, are you going to get it right?

Maybe we should ban the use of potentially offensive colloquialisms entirely? It would be much easier if these troublesome users would go elsewhere or learn to write proper English. The snob in me has already complained bitterly elsewhere in this book about crimes against the English language but it is just snobbery on my part. I don't use social media any longer and live quite happily without it. If I have something to say I can write a book or argue my case in court. However, I'm lucky to have those options. Other people's talents lie in other directions and social media provides an avenue for them to have their say as well, using the language they're comfortable with. It democratises communication and gives a voice to people who wouldn't otherwise have one and whose communication styles may make certain elites uncomfortable.

In general, bad grammar, foul language and casual affectionate insults are what T&S people get paid to deal with. They're problems for front-line content moderators and the people writing policy but using them doesn't always mean that the perpetrators are necessarily bad people. Such language doesn't always lead to wars, hate crimes, epidemics of self-harm or other issues that concern wider society either.

Elitism, us-and-them narratives and tribalism are genuine social problems. They exist independently of social media and they exist among elites as much as they do among the barbarians. They can be expressed explicitly, through the use of slurs and so forth, and can also be implied more subtly (or even just assumed in the opinions and values we express). The more skilled the communicator, the more insidious they may be and it would be wrong to cast the content moderation debate simply in terms of good people preventing the misguided or uneducated from doing harm.

Nevertheless, that is what is happening around the world. Debates, regulation, the efforts by social media companies themselves and the calls for more moderation mostly emanate from a particular class of people who share a level of privilege and educational attainment and want to change society, even if they don't agree about what change they want. Their everyday communication contains as much inherent prejudice and intolerance as the people they criticise but the only time I've heard that explicitly acknowledged was by a researcher at one seminar who proclaimed, 'We are the establishment'.

He went on to list the common characteristics of the keepers of knowledge, the people who get to decide what's true and what isn't and the gatekeepers of power. He added, quite succinctly, that if you're not a part of that elite, and that elite is not acknowledging your voice, wouldn't you be hostile to it?

This is sometimes referred to as a crisis of legitimacy. In the years following the global financial crisis of 2008, the BBC journalist Mark Mardell wrote repeatedly about what he called 'the disconnect', the perceived gap between the ruled and the rulers. Resentment at the disconnect manifested itself initially with the Occupy movement, and then a few years later with the Brexit vote in the UK and the election of Donald Trump in the US.

Facebook and other social media companies along with the T&S industry as a whole, have inadvertently created a new disconnect by labelling themselves as the smartest people in the room and claiming the privilege of deciding what communication styles are acceptable. The never-ending policy creep has led to a perception of overreach by the powerful, of a secret agenda, censorship and favouritism, when the goal is often just to protect the vulnerable or simply turn a profit. It's all a bit of a mess and the T&S industry has grown into a powerful lobby group in its own right that is heavily invested in maintaining the status quo, so the chances of reform are fading.

The other side of the coin from policy creep is the free speech argument. The United Nations considers this to be a basic human right, influenced by the first amendment of the Constitution of the United States, which says: 'Congress shall make no law respecting an establishment of religion, or prohibiting the free exercise thereof; *or abridging the freedom of speech* [my italics], or of the press; or the right of the people peaceably to assemble, and to petition the Government for a redress of grievances.'

The influence of US law in the debate about content moderation cannot be overemphasised. Facebook is a US company subject to US law, run by people who have grown up with or become accustomed to the values and principles of that country and are mostly concerned with public opinion and regulatory scrutiny in the United States. While a lot of people object to this state of affairs on general principle, the reality is that a more fragmented approach could be much worse.

In the absence of one clear framework, governments would each create their own. Every time you post anything, Facebook would have to record your location so they knew who had jurisdiction over you at that moment. What would stop a government from making their laws retrospective so that everything you've ever said on social media and every image you've ever posted would become subject to their approval the moment you set foot in their country? Or as soon as you interact with someone in their country?

Let's not forget that although attitudes and laws change over time, the record of what we say and do is permanent. Many of us have been embarrassed when workmates have found evidence of youthful indiscretions, and we constantly see public figures at the centre of a storm over some ill-considered remark made years ago. I don't want some random government making it their business to judge what I said decades ago, now or in the far future.

The question of US-centric thinking is less of a problem than the issue that, even within the United States, there is no consensus about personal freedoms and how much individuals should give up those freedoms, whether for the common good or in deference to some moral code. No matter what the rules are, there will always be huge numbers of people who disagree vehemently with them.

This tension over what people should be allowed to say is pretty much unresolvable. Content moderation exists because we live in a diverse world in which people have widely varying opinions about what is okay and what isn't. We have different values which are often rooted in different understandings of how the world works, what's important and what's true. Something that makes perfect sense to someone raised in a liberal Western tradition may be completely unacceptable to someone from a different cultural background, and vice versa.

At the end of the day, someone just has to say, 'These are the rules on this site and if you don't like them you should go somewhere else'. This is what we did on Forumosa. Facebook, like most global corporations, struggles to make an explicit statement like this because they want to define themselves as serving everyone equally. They're trying to appeal to all of the people all of the time – something that's more or less impossible in a diverse world – and the only problem is that they haven't figured out how to do content moderation well enough yet, which is equally true of the politicians and campaign groups that criticise them. To be clear, I am not letting Facebook off the hook. I just don't have a lot of confidence in government to do the job any better.

Politicians don't want to do the hard work of writing detailed rules or taking responsibility whenever there is a failure. For a politician, regulating free speech on the internet is poison. Whatever you put in, whatever you leave out, people will complain. Every decision, every inclusion, every omission is an opportunity for your enemies to criticise and attack you, or for your constituents to be outraged. It's easy to give grandiose speeches attacking big tech and demand that social media companies 'do more' but none of our elected representatives has an interest in doing the hard work that's necessary or putting themselves in the firing line. They prefer to leave it to private industry, and I suppose that's as good a solution as any.

Corporations are no more vulnerable to moral panics or special interest groups than politicians are, or should I say they are just as vulnerable but more likely to hire decent, intelligent people with no political agenda or affiliations. If we have more transparency about a corporation's motivations and interests, it can probably do the job more effectively than government can. They have a vested interest in creating a safe welcoming space where people can express themselves freely, so why not be transparent about that?

This brings me to the vexing question of whether Facebook have figured out how to do content moderation well enough yet.

It's hard to be sure without access to Facebook's internal statistics, but my general feeling on this is that by and large they haven't done too bad a job. I spent nearly a year of my life immersed in the detail of Facebook policies and it was quite rare to be in a situation where I disagreed vehemently with the general spirit, or even the detail, of a policy.

I did sometimes wish that the rule were different but could understand the reasoning behind it and see that it had been thought through and designed to be generally acceptable to the majority of people. I often quibbled about some minor point or questioned some nuance, but these were the things that were regularly tweaked as the policy team refined the wording. The result was never perfect in my eyes, but it probably wasn't perfect in the eyes of the people writing it either. There are always compromises, and the document I worked with was good enough for us all to get along together with a little bit of give and take.

Of course, the rules and the enforcement of the rules are two different things, and in 2019 the writer Mike Masnick wrote an article for *Tech Dirt* in which he postulated 'Masnick's Impossibility Theorem', which can be summed up as 'Nobody will ever do content moderation perfectly'. If you have two billion people using your platform, it only takes a very small percentage of them to break the rules and suddenly you have a massive problem (in absolute terms) on your hands.

The rule-breaking can be deliberate, it can be accidental because the user genuinely didn't realise they were doing something that's not allowed or the content can be okay but still need someone to look at it and make a decision. A fair percentage of all the content I reviewed at Facebook had been reported by someone who was offended by it but didn't actually break the rules. My job was not to go around deleting content: it was to look at stuff that might be violating and make a determination. Very often it didn't get deleted because I didn't think it had broken the rules, even if it was offensive to me or someone else.

Then, regardless of whether I had deleted it or not, someone at the other end of that process, a user, would have an opinion. They would disagree with me.

If I had deleted a post because the incorrect placement of a comma changed the meaning slightly from what was intended, so that it was now in violation of Facebook's rules, the user would disagree with that decision. If they genuinely believed that Adolf Hitler was a hero, that vegans are idiots, that it's okay to sell puppies on Facebook, that Welsh people can safely be described as 'sheep-shaggers' or that they owned their own bodies and were entitled to share photographs of their bare breasts, they might find themselves looking at a notice saying that one of their posts had been deleted.

Or not. Posting photos of your breasts is okay if you're a man, or a woman at a political protest, or in a medical context or if your nipples are at least partially covered, no matter who complains. (Interestingly, a single hair, or even a shadow, can count as partial covering.) Referring to Welsh people as sheep-shaggers was permitted while I was at Facebook, whereas describing Muslim people as having sexual relations with goats was a 'designated dehumanising comparison' and considered to be hate speech which I was required to delete.

Being offended is not grounds for deleting a post, it has to meet objective criteria, but that doesn't stop people from reporting stuff they don't like. From billions of users making billions of posts, we get millions of items being reported every day and it's inevitable that some of the moderating decisions will generate complaints from users. Those complaints all get investigated in turn, the original decision gets reviewed and sometimes it gets overturned. This in turn means that the original moderator has made a mistake.

Mistakes happen, it's part of life, especially when you're applying complex rules to human behaviour a hundred times per hour as I was. The required quality standard, 98 per cent, was very hard for most people to reach consistently, so it's safe to assume every moderator is making a handful of mistakes every hour. From those millions of decisions being made every day, there will be thousands or tens of thousands of occasions when someone has grounds to complain that their voice has been unfairly silenced, that their people are being insulted on Facebook and that Facebook has made a mistake.

Tens or hundreds of thousands of content moderation failures every day.

Most of these issues are resolved at the first appeal, but a small percentage of them slip through the net and some of those blow up into issues that become huge public relations disasters for Facebook. Sometimes the moderator's decision is at fault and sometimes the moderating decision is consistent with the rules but some detail of the rules is at odds with public opinion or common sense, resulting in a hasty change to the wording of the policy, which in turn may cause problems in future. For example, in October 2017 we were told in an urgent special advisory that the phrase 'stupid man' should be considered hate speech and deleted because it coupled a derogatory claim about someone with reference to their gender, which is a protected characteristic. That advice was rescinded after only three days, by which time I had processed over 2,000 tickets.

The mistakes get rectified and the rules get tweaked but the mistakes keep coming. From billions of posts, millions of reports and tens of thousands of mistakes, it's not realistic to expect that there will never be instances of Facebook getting it wrong. Content moderation will never be completely free of mistakes and the system will never be perfect because we're dealing with the vagaries of changing values, ideas and interpretations across hundreds of languages in diverse cultures.

Sadly, nobody gets to hear about the tens of millions of correct decisions made every day; they only hear about the latest shocking screw-up and assume that's the only thing 40,000 moderators have done that week. Just as millions of people can fly on commercial airlines every day and the public notice only the few rare disasters, billions of people use Facebook every day without incident while the perception persists that content moderation is not effective.

This was the world I was stepping into, the thankless task I was taking on, the unsolvable conundrum that was starting to dominate my life as summer 2017 turned to autumn and I embraced the next phase of my life as a Facebook contractor.

FOUR

HIGH PRIORITY
AND LOW QUALITY

September 2017 was a time of great change for us, not only for those of us working on the evening shift at Facebook but also for me and my wife in our home life. Facebook had decided that GC4, the headquarters building in Dublin, was too small for all the new people they were hiring, or else they just didn't want the plebs rubbing shoulders with the important people. While at GC4, CMs were given differently coloured ID badges, were not allowed the same access to perks as Facebook's full-time employees and were told never to make eye contact with them. Whatever the reason, we were relocated to the Beckett Building, a big office block in the old docklands on the north side of the River Liffey, which Facebook had refurbished for our use.

It was one of those buildings put up during the Celtic Tiger years, part of the earlier phase of renewal in Dublin's old docklands, which all came screeching to a halt when the global financial crisis plunged Ireland's economy into a steep recession. Now, after standing empty since it was completed a decade earlier, it was very nearly a Silicon Valley tech office.

It didn't have any logo outside, nothing to identify it as a Facebook site, but it was a nice building.

It was all glass on the outside, while the few internal walls were decorated with massive smiling emojis. I'm not sure whether they were just tacky or faintly Orwellian, but I don't think anyone liked them. Still, the whole place was bright and airy, and even if there was no table football and the desks seemed to be slightly smaller than those we had left behind, at least the air-con worked properly.

There were the same beautiful mini-kitchen areas, although these had fewer shelves of goodies, and they weren't replenished as often. We on the evening shift often had to do without a full selection of protein bars and energy drinks, and the canteen kitchen wasn't finished either. All food was prepared at GC4 and transported over, so there was inevitably a drop in both quality and quantity. It was still free food, but like everything else it seemed like a slightly poorer version of the amenities that had been part of our working life – the benefits package we had all signed up for.

Although there was a bit of disappointment, all the grumbles were over relatively small things. We liked the building well enough and it was ours. It was a moderating centre, not a shared office space, and we were happy to be able to settle in. They even let us have polls to choose the names of the meeting rooms, so instead of 'Mother of Dragons' and 'Not Angry, Just Disappointed' they now had sensible names that meant something to us.[†]

† Such as 'Wubbalubbadubdub'

My wife and I were looking for a new place to live at the same time that we moved to the new office and decided that we would rather pay city centre rents than live further out and have to commute. For one thing, my shift finished at 2 a.m. and travelling home across the city at that time didn't sound like a lot of fun. Plus, the company offered a per diem payment because there were no buses in the middle of the night and we decided to use this extra money towards our rental costs. We found a lovely, but hideously expensive, apartment within easy walking distance of our new workplace and spent a lot of time and money to turn it into a real, long-term home.

As we moved into the new office, we also transitioned to new ways of working. The chaotic collegiate atmosphere of the evening shift gave way to permanent structures and management systems. We were organised into market teams based on language and culture, sitting together, working and training to the same standard, and we got a permanent TL. Up to that point, we had been relying on an ever-changing crowd of TLs on duty, seconded for a week or two at a time from their usual roles with the day shift. Now we became Eve10, UKI (UK and Ireland) and had a permanent TL, 'Damien', who had been specifically recruited to be our full-time line manager.

Damien had previously worked managing a customer service team for a telecoms company call centre and had zero experience in content moderation. He had never done the work and hadn't even done the training. He was just there to keep us all in line and make sure we made our numbers, the poor sod. Despite Damien's role in the events of this chapter, I don't bear him any ill will. I don't think any of us knew what we were getting into when we started. I talked to him after we had both left the job, and he described it as 'mental torture' that made him feel like a puppet. He was so drained from doing it that he became a truck driver afterwards, a complete change of direction.

It's as if CPL had a policy of putting people into roles they needed to fill even if they were the wrong people. The mentality seemed to be that they would keep hammering square pegs into round holes until they either fit or broke and to make everybody do things their way regardless of whether they could or whether it was a good idea. Ultimately it's an extension of Facebook's command and control mentality, whereby everybody was just expected to do as they were told and not question the higher powers.

One of the first things that happened at work, which turned out to be rather cool, was that we all had to have 'sitting in a chair' lessons. As the shift started, we were warned that the 'ergonomics team' were coming and we had to co-operate with them, at which everyone rolled their eyes, and TL Damien said something to the effect of 'Just go along with it and they'll be out of our hair quicker.' Nobody was excited or committed.

A few hours later, there was a tap on my shoulder and I tried to convey just the right amount of polite irritation and resignation as I took off my headset to talk to a very professional young woman who started insistently prodding and tweaking my posture. She changed all the settings on my chair, adjusted the monitor, made me slide a support under my wrist and a footrest under the desk and generally made me feel like an idiot. But I did feel a lot more comfortable.

It was amazing how big a difference all those little changes made. I was suddenly aware of the tension I was carrying in my shoulders, the slight discomfort in my back and all the other little things we put up with every day and stop noticing. For fifty years I had been flopping into whatever random piece of furniture the world offered me without really thinking about it, and only then did I understand what I had been doing to myself. This was amazing!

If only this had been my permanent desk; it really could have been transformational. Unfortunately, the next morning someone else used the desk and chair and changed everything. It wasn't long before chairs got swapped around, and my footrest got kicked to one side and then into a corner where I eventually found it, broken. Trying to put everything back the way I liked it at the start of my shift became a chore, the urgency of the lesson receded and soon things were back to the way they had been. (The first thing I did when I started writing this book was to go out and buy a good-quality office chair. I picked a place with a big table to serve as my desk, set up a stand to put my screen at the appropriate height and so on. I did learn from the lesson I was given and appreciate the trouble and expense that Facebook went to on our behalf. So that was a positive.)

Sadly, although the professionals they sent to take care of us seemed to be competent and committed, the HR person responsible was just ticking a box. They provided ergonomics support and didn't stop to think about how we would be able to implement anything in a hot-desking environment. I think, as with 'wellness', this was something that someone higher up felt was important but the implementation was delegated to someone who wasn't thinking and the result was a waste of everyone's time.

I had my first real encounter with the wellness team at about the time we moved to Beckett as well. I guess we had had some compulsory resilience training in groups by then (which was sitting around a conference table doing breathing exercises with someone who had no idea what our work entailed) but some time in September I requested a one-to-one counselling session.

This wasn't because I was feeling traumatised by extreme content; I just had a lot on my plate and nobody I could easily talk to. My wife was far from her own country and family and had a little friction with a few members of her community in Ireland. It was no big deal, but I had become very aware that I was her entire support network at the same time as I realised I didn't have one of my own.

I had some dramas with my own family to take care of. I was new in Ireland and didn't know anybody except for my colleagues, and this was my first time working in a corporate environment. I could feel that I didn't fit in, and I had a variety of small stresses to deal with and a free resource to take advantage of. Why not spend half an hour seeing what I could learn if my employer was paying for it?

I don't recall the session being especially useful; I didn't get any great insights or life-changing advice. I felt that I had wasted my time looking for guidance from someone with basically no life experience. However, no harm was done, and there was one moment in the session which stuck in my mind afterwards and is relevant even today.

I don't remember what prompted me to say this, and I don't think I was feeling especially stressed about the content I was seeing at the time, but I said to the counsellor that she was in a uniquely privileged situation to study and understand the long-term impacts of doing this job. It seemed to me that for somebody in the wellness industry this would be a new and exciting emerging field. I assumed that she would be keen to better understand and document the stresses associated with this unique working environment but she replied that she didn't think Facebook would want anybody publishing anything that might make them look bad. I wouldn't go so far as to say that she was alarmed at my suggestion but I had obviously touched on a taboo subject.

The UKI team mostly worked on high-priority content – the stuff that needs to be dealt with quickly – but we also did other work. On a typical evening, I would see maybe 50 new user accounts that seemed suspicious and amuse myself with the weird and wonderful identity documents they submitted.

That was what I did when I needed a bit of light relief; the rest of the time I was just slogging through the nasty shit.

If you as a user see something on Facebook or Instagram that you think shouldn't be there, you can report it by clicking on the appropriate link. And then you'll see a screen asking you why you're reporting it. You can select the option to say it's porn or graphic violence, whatever you think the problem is. If you see something posted by a user in the UK or Ireland and label it as graphic violence it goes into the high-priority queue to be reviewed by me, my colleagues or the guys on the day shift.

Typically, the high-pri (high-priority) queue would have 20,000 or more tickets waiting to be processed at the start of my shift, after the day shift had spent all day trying to clear the backlog. We called them tickets, I guess because the people who designed the system came from a customer support background where customer requests were referred to as tickets. The work of content moderation today is completely different from working in a call centre, but the systems and language used to describe our work – and therefore the way we think about the work – remain the same. We were managed like call centre workers, and nothing mattered except meeting our targets. Damien was supported by his anchor mentor (AM) James the Frapist (the same guy that had once tried to use my computer to access the secure internal network and had somehow now been magically promoted). His job at the start of the evening was to look at the queues and assign work to each of us via the game plan (GP) to ensure that nothing went over turnaround time (TAT), the interval between the report by the user and us dealing with it. For the high-pri queue, the maximum TAT was 48 hours. I think there were a couple of more urgent queues with a TAT of 24 hours. The regular stuff was expected to be dealt with in anything between three and five days.

More content is reported when the world sits down to goof off on Facebook in the evening after work or if there has been a high-profile event that everyone has an opinion about. The queues were represented graphically, so this trend would show up as a peak on the graph. As time went on that peak would move closer to the TAT deadline, and it's the AM's job to anticipate these surges and ensure enough people are working the appropriate queue at the appropriate time to prevent it from going over TAT.

I would sit down at my desk and open the GP, which is an Excel spreadsheet filled in by the AM on a shared-access service provided by some outside company. (At the time I wondered why one of the world's largest tech companies was relying on, and posting sensitive data to, an outside company. I think the answer is that nobody at Facebook knew or cared how we did our work enough to provide a more appropriate tool.) This spreadsheet listed everyone's work assignments, and I would go from there to an internal web page called single review tool (SRT) and click 'just go' on the high-pri queue.

The first ticket would load in front of me immediately. It was that simple. I would see the offending content, the names of the user who posted it and whoever reported it and be expected to make a decision immediately using the number pad on my keyboard.

It was very simple: option 1 to ignore it, option 2 to delete it, and others to mark it as disturbing, escalate to the safety team etc. If you chose option 1 you would be asked to choose again between option 1>>1: 'ignore as benign' and option 1>>2: 'ignore but mark as sexually suggestive'.

Choose option 2, sexually suggestive, and you would get a list of 30-plus definitions for sexually suggestive and have to choose the most appropriate one. Option 1>>2>>9, I remember, was for a woman's cleavage. This was not the same as a woman in a bikini and was further up the hierarchy. If a woman is wearing a bikini and also displaying cleavage, you chose the key combination 1>>2>>9 and not 1>>2>>C (the combination for a bikini).†

Very often, content would be reported for one reason and we would find nothing wrong with it under the relevant rules but then have to action it under the sexually suggestive rules anyway. This was all to identify content which would be disapproved of in more conservative cultures, even though it was perfectly acceptable to us and the people running

---

† There seemed to be more definitions of sexually suggestive content involving women than there were involving men but we did have a category for phallic objects, such as cakes or mushrooms that looked like male genitalia, so I guess the policy team were trying to be fair.

Facebook. It wouldn't be deleted, just maybe hidden in Saudi Arabia or Alabama.

Then of course there was all the content that Facebook didn't want on their platform. You might find yourself looking at something, pressing option 2 to delete it and then navigating through several more layers to find the choice you wanted. For example: delete>> category adult nudity>> subcategory sexual content>> subcategory penises>> subcategory erections (rather than >> subcategory flaccid penis). In hindsight, I can see just how surreal this was but at the time we just accepted it. It seemed perfectly normal to have serious discussions about how visible a nipple was or what counted as actually erect. It seems like insanity today and although I can see the reasons for it, it's still incredible to me that this was how I spent my time.

To make a decision all I needed was the number pad on my keyboard. I would navigate through the process by simply typing, for example, 2417 <enter>, and the content would vanish from my screen to be replaced by the next item in the queue. The whole process usually took just a few seconds, then you did it again and again. And again. There was no pause between tickets. As soon as you worked one, the next one would be right there waiting for you. It was relentless.

We were mostly free to manage our own time in those days as long as we hit our targets. I would typically work 100 tickets per hour, which usually allowed me to take a ten-minute break before diving back in. You might get 10 or 20 tickets in a row that were super easy to deal with and once you're in the groove you can blast through them, taking just a few seconds each time. Then you get something which required some deeper analysis and might take several minutes to study and think through. Over an hour or so, it averaged out that I was within the specified average handling time (AHT), another of the metrics which was listed on the GP. For the high-pri queue, the AHT was supposed to be 30 seconds, which was about right.

Six or seven hours of this, and I would achieve the GP target for the night and everybody would be mostly happy. However, it was gruelling and, even with regular breaks, it seemed like we never had time to decompress or process anything.

I would often work a ticket, move on and work several more, then have second thoughts and scroll back through my workflow to revise a particular decision. I was not forgetting the content the instant it was replaced on the screen by something else. Our heads were full of images and words; they were there swirling around inside us even as we were cramming more in.

Part of the problem was the Hierarchy, Facebook's system for prioritising what to worry about. This was hugely important. Spam was the most important thing to watch out for, above even child pornography or terrorist threats. It was also more important than hate speech or live-streaming a suicide because of the amount of it. Even today, a quick look at Facebook's transparency report shows that in Q4 of 2021 they deleted 17.4 million items that were considered hate speech, compared with 1.2 billion pieces of spam.

Among other oddities, female nipples were more serious than threatening to rape someone. Threatening to kill someone could fall under any one of several different policies, depending on semantics. A pile of naked dead bodies might be deleted in some circumstances or marked as sexually suggestive in others. If they died as a result of violence we marked it as disturbing, unless there was a violating caption.† However, in these cases, the 'newsworthy' exception could be applied. Then everything changed again.

If you took the right action for the wrong reason then that was classed as a mistake. If someone posted an image of a naked man in an ad to sell fake sunglasses to raise money for the Judean People's Front then the questions to ask would be, in order:

- Does clicking this link take me to a page that attempts to steal my personal data?
- Are those sunglasses on the list of brands we protect?
- Is the Judean People's Front listed as a terrorist organisation?
- Can I see his soft bits?

Delete the naked man for being naked when his real crime is harming Gucci's profits, and you're in trouble.

---

† A violating caption is text accompanying an image that changes its status from acceptable to a violation. For example, a picture of a teenage boy with a broken leg is fine on its face, but add a caption that says 'serves him right' and it could violate the rules.

Aside from us regular content moderators, there were also strange semi-mythical beings called auditors, who were tasked with checking everyone's work. Some automated system would take a random selection of the tickets we worked and send them to a special queue where the auditor would take a look and make their own decisions about how to deal with the ticket. They wouldn't know who else had already worked the ticket or what decision they had made. Their workflow was the same as ours but if there was a discrepancy between their decision and mine then the system would assume that the auditor was correct. I would then get a quality mistake notification on my dashboard and would have to send a message to try and negotiate with them to 'get the point back'.

This kind of system probably worked just fine for people whose job was to check identity documents. There was very little to interpret, with few grey areas, and deciding the right action was pretty clear-cut. Often, but not always, there was a flowchart to follow. The required quality target of 98 per cent seemed reasonable. If your auditor reviews a hundred of your decisions and disagrees with you more than once or twice then maybe you need some more training as it's fair to say that you might be doing something wrong.

Content moderation is much more nuanced and problematic. There are so many edge cases and so much room for interpretation that disagreements happen all the time. We used to keep a UKI group chat open while working and anyone who wasn't sure about the right action on something would post the ticket number there for everyone else to take a look. It was in constant use and there were a lot of discussions and opinions about all sorts of different content. It was common to see two or three people standing around a screen together, pointing out details in the content and looking at different parts of the IS to try and get clarity.

For example, in October 2017 someone rented a hotel room in Las Vegas overlooking the venue of an outdoor concert. They took a bag full of guns up there with them and started shooting indiscriminately into the crowd. The next night I saw a meme depicting someone pointing an assault rifle out of a window, with a caption about what to do if the kids down the road are playing their music too loud. It seemed to me that this was a reference to the previous day's events and was trying to make some kind of joke at the expense of the victims. I wasn't sure so I asked my colleagues and their opinions were split. Some said it was fine; some said to delete it.

In this situation we are supposed to put a post on the UKI tribe – basically a Facebook group in the secret Workplace area – and provide a description with a link to the ticket. The idea was that one of the auditors or trainers would look at it and give some guidance, but they all worked on the day shift and wouldn't see it for another 12 hours. In the meantime, we were not allowed to skip tickets because if they weren't processed they would go over TAT and this meant our productivity metrics would suffer. I had to make my own decision and live with the consequences if I got it wrong.

I took a deep breath and deleted the ticket. Half an hour later it came up again. And again. And again. I think I saw that same image maybe 11 times that night, and despite not knowing what to do or having anybody further up the food chain that I could ask, I had to deal with it each time. I wasn't the only one seeing it either; everyone on the team saw it again and again and had to make their own judgement call about what to do with it. Some deleted it; some didn't.

The next evening, I sat down at my desk at 6 o'clock and there was a notification on my dashboard that I had been audited. For some reason, the supposedly random system had asked my auditor to review seven instances of the same content and he had ruled seven times that I had made the wrong decision. So I was sitting there staring at seven quality mistakes at the start of my shift.

To put this in perspective, the monthly audit sample was supposed to be 200 to 250 tickets in total. To meet the 98 per cent quality target, you were only allowed a maximum of five mistakes in a month. Here we were at the start of the month and I had already blown past that limit!

There was also a reply in the tribe explaining the auditor's thinking, which was that the meme had not explicitly referenced the shooting so had to be viewed just as a general comment. I could see that I wasn't going to win that argument but to be punished multiple times for one mistake seemed harsh. TL Damien tried to get my numbers adjusted, without success. The system was remorseless and there was no leeway or flexibility even when the outcome was counterproductive.

There's no way to make Facebook aware of this. Someone in an ivory tower at MPK creates rules and hands them off to outside contractors whose key performance indicator is compliance. In the same way that they require contractors to provide ergonomics support or wellness counselling, they provide a list of what to allow and what to take down and then don't take any further interest in what's going on. They only measure how well we do what we are told, not whether they're making compliance easy for us or whether compliance is going to help them reach their goals in moderating the platform. It's as if Facebook believes that their sole duty is to produce documents describing the things they don't want to see and that everything after that is someone else's problem.

In 2017, when I was hired, Mark Zuckerberg stated that 4,500 people were working on T&S for Facebook worldwide. In 2019 he claimed that number was 30,000, and it has gone up again since then to 40,000. He has ten times more people doing the work, and they're supported by an AI that is supposed to be handling a lot of the more straightforward cases. The IS is a much more refined document today. However, despite the numerous tweaks they have made to their systems, the problem of extreme content is far worse today than it was in 2017.

FIVE

EVERYDAY PEOPLE

t's common for journalists to focus on graphic imagery when talking about content moderation but, to be honest, a great deal of the work revolved around written text and a lot of it was quite mundane. People say awful shit online every day and we worked under a constant deluge of nastiness, hatred, lies and small-mindedness that was just as debilitating over time as the images that might be easier for you to visualise.

I've tried to talk about this publicly, but it doesn't make for as good a story. In some cases, I've even had to argue with 'experts' – people who have never done the work but whose careers have been advanced by documenting stories about how moderators see blood and gore and unspeakable violence all day long. The truth is, graphic images are only part of the job.

Imagine two people, let's call them Peter and Jane, who have been in a relationship that has now ended. Maybe one or both already has a child from a previous relationship, and/or they have a child together. Neither of them is a perfect and enlightened individual. Their lives are stressful and unhappy, they've made mistakes and have insecurities just like the rest of us and all of this manifests itself in their online bickering. One thinks the other is not a good parent, one accuses the other of infidelity or sexual behaviours they feel entitled to criticise, one is allegedly a drunkard or a junkie and so on.

Take your pick: the claims and judgements and accusations are flying backwards and forwards. Someone's mother gets involved. Someone's new or previous partner wants to have their say. Everyone is emotional and wants to win or to hurt someone else and soon the comments start getting reported.

The reporting tool is a weapon for the weak, and all too often for the small-minded. (Consider the fact that 22% of the content reported as Covid misinformation in 2020 was reported in the middle of an argument by individuals who appeared to be doing it out of spite.) As comments started appearing in the queue I was working, there were several of us working those tickets, all seeing disconnected bits of the argument. We didn't get to see the whole thing from start to finish, only the individual comments in our own tickets. They were written by people with no interest in punctuation, grammar or spelling. We would have to go through each one line by line, clause by clause – every subject-verb-object combination – and identify every single violation, usually of the bullying policy. You can't call her that, you can't say that about him, that claim is permitted, this one is okay because it wasn't reported by the person it's talking about but by his mother, you can't use that word, oh for fuck's sake, get a life! Now, which violation was furthest up the hierarchy?

It's incredibly depressing to read this stuff. I found it quite exhausting going through it with a fine toothcomb to identify all the violations so that I could choose the most important one as defined by the hierarchy of actions. If I had been given any free will, I would have deleted the whole lot for crimes against the English language.

Does that sound extreme and intolerant? It gets worse.

One evening, one of my colleagues asked me if I thought I was becoming more racist. I shrugged because I hadn't thought about it and asked why. He replied that all the racist comments he was reading were starting to make sense to him and sound persuasive. This was quite a serious thing to think about, especially as I am married to an immigrant person of colour who was raised as a Muslim. The idea that I might be being brainwashed by racist rhetoric was quite scary.

Not so long ago I had some interesting conversations with a former CM – someone from a minority background themselves – who seemed to be permanently angry about what they perceived as a liberal bias in Facebook's policies. They were openly contemptuous about some of the minorities the rules are there to protect and complained about political correctness. This is not a good place to be discussing the validity or otherwise of their perspectives, but I think it's important to recognise that they were out of step with the values of the organisation they were representing. How did a person like this come to be employed for several years in this role if they disagreed so vehemently with what the role entails?

Or had their opinions and values been shaped by the work over time?

In June 2017 a man named Darren Osborne rented a van and drove it through a crowd of people outside a mosque at Finsbury Park in London. One man died, others were injured and Osborne ended up in prison. The police investigation concluded that he had been at risk and emotionally vulnerable as a result of life events and had then immersed himself in racist propaganda. He binge-watched content by right-wing commentators like Tommy Robinson and a group called Britain First and was described by the police in court as 'brainwashed' by it. The people he harmed in his attack were not the only victims: Osborne himself was also a victim of the same content that we were watching every day in huge quantities.

Britain First and Tommy Fucking Robinson were there on our screens every day saying things that others found objectionable and reported. We would have to look at and listen to their arguments and then apply Facebook's rules to see if they had said anything that required us to delete the content. It was very rare that they actually broke the rules. They had mastered the art of spreading hatred and intolerance while still being technically innocent of anything. We would think about what they were saying, then shrug and say, 'That's okay, option 1.1, ignore, benign'. The content would stay up, then someone else would see it and report it, and we would have to review it again.

How many times can you hear the same argument, think about it, apply the best guidance you can get from highly paid experts and conclude that they're not saying anything wrong without it starting to affect you? You may have noticed that I sound quite sympathetic to the white British man I describe as a victim and have very little to say about all the people he harmed or killed. I'd like to say that that's simply a narrative choice, a way of making a point, but I no longer trust my judgement or motivations.

Britain First were eventually banned from Facebook just before I left the job. The official statement claimed that it was because they had repeatedly broken the rules. Delighted as we were with the decision – it got a round of applause in the office – we couldn't help reminding each other that BF never broke the rules.

—

Within a week or two of the move to Beckett and the formation of market teams on the evening shift, we started to get some very troubling feedback.

We were being audited properly for the first time, and apparently, we weren't reaching the required quality target. First, we had team meetings where we were told we needed to raise our game and then some of the auditors, who all worked on the day shift, started to occasionally stay back for an hour or two and give us additional training. In conversations – and arguments – with them, it started to become clear that very often the right answer depended on the interpretation of the content and that was quite subjective. The right answer was a matter of opinion.

These meetings were sometimes a bit tense because they were our first face-to-face interactions with people whose auditing decisions we didn't always agree with. But as we got to know one another we got better at discussing the issues and started to win appeals about audits. Although this helped with our quality scores, I couldn't help questioning the validity of the process. If I could get the point back three times out of four, did that not mean that my auditor was wrong three-quarters of the time?

I started to suspect that the only reason the day shift had better quality scores was that the auditors were part of that team and it was just easier for everyone to be on the same page because they were all sitting together and constantly discussing their decisions with each other. We did the same thing on the evening shift, but the consensus we reached was sometimes a bit different from the day shift. It was possible that if we were audited by people who worked the same hours as us then we would have similar quality scores to the day shift, but nobody on the evening shift was able to become an auditor because our quality scores were too low!

At about this time we started to see the first firings. There would be hints in conversation that people were struggling and then one day they would just not be there any more. They would just disappear without any explanation and never be mentioned again. At the time that seemed fair enough. In any group of people, especially if they were hired without a lot of consideration, you will probably get a few who are in the wrong role. However, if everybody on the team is failing, either there is something wrong with the way they're being trained and managed or else you have unreasonable expectations of them. By this I mean that there is some systemic problem with your hiring practices which causes you to hire only unsuitable people.

At that point, somebody decided it would be a good idea to have everyone on Eve10 do regular quizzes created by people on the day team, something that made me groan quietly in horror. For one thing, quizzes are a simple way to test whether your students have absorbed rote information but they're not a good tool for evaluating how people interpret complex content. For another, quiz design is a complex and skilled process. (I talked to a teacher friend who was responsible for the entire testing regime in a university department with 90 lecturers and they were horrified by what was going on in my workplace.) Unfortunately, the people creating the quizzes were just doing what they had been told and didn't know any better than to base the questions on the most difficult and controversial content they had recently encountered.

Several of the people tasked with helping us had only been in the job a month or two longer than we had. They had no training or support but had been saddled with fixing a problem that I believe was just an artefact of the auditing process and the management system.

Since the quizzes were not representative of our regular work and not created by anyone with a background in education, the results were predictably ridiculous. I remember occasions when I scored 100 per cent in one quiz, the only person in my team to do so, but was bottom of the rankings in the next one. I remember my whole team protesting about certain questions and arguing successfully that the official right answer was actually the wrong answer. It was farcical.

Worst of all, there were people with better-than-average quality scores in their actual work who happened to score low in one of these stupid quizzes and were then told they were no longer permitted to do the important and difficult work on the high-pri queue. The whole thing started to smell of panic. It seemed like nobody higher up knew how to solve the problem or even think objectively about what the problem was.

It wasn't really their fault: they were just everyday people being subjected to unreasonable pressure to achieve goals that hadn't been thought out. It was as if Facebook had just written a rule book and ordered our managers to apply it to an unattainable standard but wasn't interested in getting any feedback on whether the system they had created was fit for purpose. They certainly didn't provide any resources as the quizzes had to be created using the free online tool SurveyMonkey.

Some time in October 2017, as part of the process of establishing our permanent functional market teams, a couple of vacancies opened up for the role of coach for Eve10. This was one rung down from being a trainer, a job which got you a pay rise of 50 cents per hour but was still seen as a promotion. The coach's job was to deliver policy updates and take a proactive role in helping the team members to maintain and improve the quality scores. It seemed like exactly the kind of exciting opportunity I was looking for: a chance to start moving up the greasy pole.

One of the key questions on the application form asked for a suggestion of something you would introduce to improve your team's quality scores. I had already figured out that Eve10's comparatively lower quality scores were an artefact created by a flawed auditing process and, to me, the obvious solution was for us to be better aligned with the day shift. My suggestion was that everyone from both day and evening shifts be encouraged to occasionally work from, say, 2 p.m. until 10 p.m. to spend time with both groups.

This was a big ask and the committee of TLs evaluating the applications didn't like the idea. I didn't even get an interview for the position and put it out of my head not long after when the whole team was pulled into a meeting to be briefed about an important upcoming event, 'the NGO', by a dynamic TL named 'Bill'.

NGO usually stands for 'non-governmental organisation' and refers to groups like Amnesty International and Greenpeace. However, in CPL's world, the NGO is an event which happens every year. Bill told us that the European Commission conducts an annual review to see how well

Facebook handles reports of hate speech and other harmful content and that civil society groups would be spending the next month scouring conversations on Facebook in search of things to report.

It was a big deal and imperative that we maintain the highest possible quality scores for the coming month. For that reason, most of our team were no longer permitted to work on high-pri content because they happened to have not done well in the latest quiz. They all protested that their actual quality scores for the work they were doing were as good as everyone else's but the powers that be remained resolutely and inscrutably stupid.

We headed back to our desks quite disturbed and dissatisfied. My immediate reaction was to try and get a better understanding of what was going on. I sat down in front of my computer, googled furiously and ten minutes later I was marvelling at the idiocy of the people I was working for. They had set a new record in the Corporate Stupidity Olympics!

The European Commission does indeed test all social media companies every year to see how quickly they respond to user reports of hate speech. They don't publish any details of how the testing is done or the mechanics of the process, but it would make sense that they might outsource the actual work to some groups – NGOs – that monitor this kind of thing anyway. Crucially, however, the European Commission does not provide a detailed set of rules and definitions about what constitutes hate speech and social media companies are not being evaluated on whether they make the 'right' decision according to some universal standard. The key metric here is TAT – turnaround time – not quality scores. They want to know whether stuff is being dealt with quickly, nothing else.

I tried to imagine what game of telephone had been played, from whoever dealt with the Commission directly all the way down to us lowly foot soldiers. The message had gone from 'go as fast as you can' to 'focus on doing it right even if it means going slowly', presumably through several variations of 'try to go faster without sacrificing quality too much'. Somewhere along the way, communications had broken down so badly that our management team had no idea what the object of the exercise was and was actively taking steps that would make it harder to reach the goal – based on quiz results from SurveyMonkey, not actual quality scores.

Instead of all hands to the pumps, most of the team had been assigned to less important work and the rest of us were told to focus on the wrong thing. I think it was about this time that I started to understand how little involvement Facebook had with the day-to-day realities of our work. Later on, when Facebook started responding publicly to criticisms I had made about them in the press, the PR people would make statements about training, support and welfare that they probably genuinely believed. They had no idea what was going on in an operation that employed 40,000 people. How do you resolve a problem with an organisation that can get things so backwards and still believe it knows everything?

Despite all the efforts that were being made, Eve10 quality scores remained stubbornly in the low 90s. However, we noticed that when we appealed auditing decisions they were very often reversed and this was a big deal. If a typical auditing sample was 200 to 250 decisions in a month, you are only allowed four to five mistakes if you wanted to meet the 98 per cent quality target. If you had ten mistakes and appealed against eight of them because you felt there was some reasonable doubt, you would often win back six.

If you had 20 mistakes, which was more common, you needed to win back more than half of them for your quality score to look respectable. Our TL, Damien, was very keen that we appeal every decision where we felt there was any chance of getting the point back. But our auditors were on the day shift and were very busy, and we weren't there with them to politely remind them that we needed an answer. We would send our appeals off into the void and all too often never get a response. To make things worse, we were only allowed to use the little feedback box on SRT, not email or chat, so we couldn't go into a lot of detail and it was easy for them to ignore us.

The rule was that appeals had to be dealt with and finalised within two weeks of the audit. After that, the record was locked and couldn't be changed, which meant your quality score for that period was now set in stone. If your auditor came back to you a day after the cut-off and told you that they had accepted your decision as the correct one after all, it was too late: your quality score had already been recorded.

I talked to Damien about this and showed him actual examples where the auditors had ultimately sided with me but it had been too late so the record in the system said I had got it wrong. I wasn't the only one it was happening to. He could see the problem and it was a problem for him as well because he was also being evaluated on how well the team did. We all wanted a resolution. He tried talking to his counterpart on the day team to get them to clear the backlog and also asked me to email a list of all my outstanding appeals, with ticket numbers, to him and the relevant point of contact (POC) on the day team.

It didn't do any good, though, and the situation dragged on through November as we plugged away at the NGO. I became increasingly stressed by it all. There were 15–20 of us on Eve10, depending on who had joined the team and who had been disappeared that week, but only three of us were allowed to work the high-pri queue – we were carrying the whole weight of the workload for the most important stuff.

High-pri was hard. That was why you needed to get a good score on the quiz before you were allowed to work that queue. There were so many more opportunities to get it wrong when you were applying nuanced policies around hate speech than if you were just identifying spam or checking for fake accounts. In addition, the auditors were paying special attention to that queue during this time. I was in this perverse situation in which I was good enough to be in the elite, whether I wanted to be or not, but then held to a higher standard because of it. We three were trying to cross a minefield every night, while the majority of our colleagues had been sent to play in a meadow nearby.

Actually, only two of us crossed the minefield every night, and I admit I was the slower one, while the other guy worked like a machine. The third? Well, I think I mentioned that the GPs were shared with the whole team, which meant everyone could see what everyone else had done every night. It became pretty clear that one of us was protecting his quality by focusing on the other queues and doing the absolute bare minimum of hi-pri work. He had figured out that it was better to be in trouble for not doing enough than it was to make the inevitable mistakes that came with the territory in hi-pri. After all, we had been told to go slow and avoid mistakes, so he had a ready-made excuse!

I called him out on it one night over a cup of tea and he just grinned at me. I was the idiot, and we both knew it, but it was too late. I had already committed and now I was dealing with the consequences of my over-eagerness. Still, it would have been nice to get more support from the auditors.

At the same time that we were being ordered to do things exactly wrong, we were still being micromanaged by the numbers. They were the wrong numbers, which was bad enough, but worse was my discovery, during my five-month review just after the NGO, that TL Damien didn't even understand how the numbers worked. He looked at my weekly quality scores instead of the monthly ones and reached the wrong conclusions.

There's a basic rule in statistics that the larger your sample the more accurate your result. Our quality scores were supposed to be calculated from a sample of at least 200 tickets and audited over the course of a month. Depending on their workload, the auditor might review 100 tickets in one week, 25 the next, etc. This means the weekly quality scores are not reliable, the sample size is often too small. You have to look at the monthly score or calculate rolling weekly scores based on the previous month.

It so happened that my quality score had been mostly pretty good, except for one week where I had been 'given' several mistakes from a small number of audits and the auditors hadn't responded to my appeals in time. Looking at my monthly average, my quality score was still just about acceptable. However, poor Damien added together the weekly percentage quality store scores instead of the hard numbers, and averaged those, pulling my score for the month down a percentage point or two.

It doesn't sound like a lot, but I couldn't afford to lose even one point in an environment where the quality target was 98 per cent, and I tried to argue with him that he was making a mistake. He didn't want to hear it and I came out of that review with an undeserved warning that I needed to up my game. As I had just spent a month going hell for leather to try and keep the high-priority queue below TAT, as a result of half my team being sidelined because of poor management decisions, I was pretty pissed off. Ironically, even though my quality score was being interpreted as too low, I was still allowed to keep working the high-pri queue because I had done well in the quizzes – much to the chagrin of James the Frapist. He was relegated to the fake Thor Odinson queues because of his quiz scores, even though he was just as competent as I was at the real work.

TL Damien had a boss who had a boss, who also had a boss, and so on. The most senior person in the building was the evening team's site manager, 'Pedro' and I figured that I wasn't going to get my quality score fixed with half measures, so I pinged him on chat and asked for five minutes of his time.

Pedro was very receptive and reasonable and grasped the problem with the quality score calculations straight away. He recalculated my score with me, there and then, using the hard numbers, and confirmed that I was right. He promised to sort it out and as I was leaving he asked me if there was anything else I could tell him.

I got the impression that he was frustrated at not knowing enough about what was going on. Maybe the reports he was receiving were being sanitised. I don't know. We talked some more about quality scores and auditing and I shared my theory that the evening shift's lower quality scores may be an artefact of the way the auditing was done. He could appreciate the argument that the day shift and evening shift needed better integration and liked my suggestion that everyone on both day and evening shifts should periodically be required to work from 2 p.m. to 10 p.m. so that we all spent time with both teams and we could harmonise our thinking. I told him that I wanted to try it that same week and he nodded.

That was, I think, on a Tuesday evening. On Wednesday I was informed by TL Damien that I and one other guy from my team would be working this hybrid shift for the next two days, Thursday and Friday. I was delighted and thoroughly enjoyed the experience, and I was present when the day shift TL put out a call for volunteers to work over the weekend. Eve10 were not allowed to work weekends because our quality scores were too low, making us miss out on the extra pay and benefits. I don't think the day shift TL knew this. Or maybe she didn't care, because when I put my hand up she accepted straight away. I felt like I had unlocked the challenge and maybe we could start to turn around the situation at last.

I never saw Pedro again. He vanished from his desk and his name was never mentioned. He just ceased to exist.

SIX

THE SMARTEST PEOPLE IN THE ROOM

This is a personal story about working in an organisation with a culture of mediocrity. However, it's also an investigation into a critical question that affects us all: when everybody has a direct communication channel with everybody else in the world, what should people be allowed to say and when is it okay to silence them? And who does the silencing?

Shortly before I took this job, a teenage girl in England committed suicide as a result of things that happened online. She wasn't the last and there will probably be more in future. CMs are the first line of defence in these situations. When I started I always strove to respond dispassionately and thoughtfully in my moderating decisions to protect the vulnerable as my priority. I'm mature and well-informed and I aspire to be a well-trained and supported professional who is emotionally stable and focused on doing the right thing.

We all know somebody young, or otherwise vulnerable, and if we suspected they were being bullied, led astray, abused or taken advantage of on Facebook, we would report it. I'm sure we would hope that the CM dealing with that report would have the time and bandwidth to process it properly and would focus on the welfare of the user before anything else.

The truth is that most CMs are young and in precarious employment. They get a few weeks of training before being thrown into the work. They're very poorly paid and on temporary contracts. The working environment is all about game plans, average handling times and quality scores. Pleasing your auditors and team leader takes precedence over solving problems and helping people. Too many mistakes and you're out. Ask too many questions and you're out. Have your own opinions, or argue about anything, and you're out.

Worst of all, the work takes a toll. Many moderators are either traumatised or at least partially brainwashed by the toxic rubbish they see all day every day. Sometimes they're traumatised *and* brainwashed. There is a huge turnover of staff. The ones who haven't left are hanging on in quiet desperation to a job they believe they need and dare not seek help in managing their mental health. If they survive long enough to get promoted, this creates a spiral staircase of inept management which has persuaded itself that everything is okay. A former TL later described this situation to me as being akin to Stockholm Syndrome.

All this leads to social media platforms failing people like you, and it happens because they are stuck. Organisations get stuck when they do things because they have always done them. Individuals become invested in the status quo, get used to doing things a particular way or simply lose track of why they're doing them, and suddenly there is a commitment to practices that don't make any sense.

Facebook's content moderation efforts are stuck. At some point, about 15 years ago, someone stepped up and took responsibility for dealing with an occasional problem, because some idiots had started insulting people or posting pictures of their penis on their profiles. They did their best to come up with some systems and solutions to handle this efficiently and make the problem go away, but it didn't work.

The problem got worse, and instead of moving fast and breaking things, they doubled down on what they were doing. People rallied around to help, budgets were increased and careers and teams were built around this new emerging specialisation. The problem got bigger, the urgency grew, the individuals and the system all leaned into the plan and questioning it came to be viewed as heresy.

Despite the ever-increasing scale of their efforts, the problem of harmful content is worse now than it has ever been. We've gone from 4,500 CMs to 40,000 and now they're also aided by artificial intelligence which does a lot of the work for them. However, even after learning all the lessons of the last five or ten years, the clamour of voices demanding that X be deleted or Y not be deleted is louder than ever.

On one hand, we have the town of Bitche in France having its social media presence cut off because Facebook didn't like its name. We have cancer awareness charities in Sweden using animations of women with square breasts because real images would get taken down and their accounts potentially closed, even though Facebook's rules explicitly allow for naked breasts in a medical context. On the other hand, we have continued and increasing harm online, proliferating hate groups and deliberate misinformation on a scale that threatens public health and social stability.

I used to wonder what kind of person you have to be to work in the upper echelons of Facebook's T&S effort and tell yourself that everything is okay. Who could read all of those stories in the press about content moderators dying at their desks, using drugs, hoarding examples of awful content and bringing lawsuits because they believe they've been harmed and dismiss it all as a little over-dramatic?

Surprisingly, those at the top of T&S seem to be perfectly reasonable and decent humans who genuinely care about solving a CM's problems. They honestly believe that they can solve them and are doing their absolute best. I have met quite a few of them at conferences, workshops and networking events for T&S professionals and have been impressed by the warmth, camaraderie, intelligence and compassion that I have encountered. It's completely at odds with what I had to deal with from my CPL managers.

I have heard these people talk openly about the cumulative effect of exposure to extreme content and the risk of trauma. Someone who had been part of the core T&S team at a big social media company during the pioneering days and had spent their days reviewing nasty stuff to decide what the rules should be described their first effort at therapy as 'listening to recordings of whale song in a darkened room'. This was at least half a decade before I joined the industry.

There is, and always was, a recognition of the potential harms inherent in the work, but somewhere between the top management and the contractors doing the work there have been another of those communication breakdowns. The people at the top are somehow divorced from what's going on at the front line and that to me is a systemic problem. It's a symptom of the dysfunctional relationship between Facebook and the contracting companies they use, the reluctance of the organisation to change, the culture of secrecy and the perverse incentives acting on those right at the very top of the power structure.

I'll explore these issues more in the coming chapters, but for now the questions to ask are these what kind of person will pick a fight with one of the world's most powerful companies, and how did I become that person?

The answer involves some biographical trivia, starting with my parents' decision to wrench me, a newly minted teenager, from our familiar parochial northern English town and transplant me into a genteel rural Welsh one instead. Looking back, it was probably a good thing they did, although I was initially none too pleased about being forced to go and live amongst the sheep-shaggers.

I was a nerdy, introspective kid, not interested in sports, new in town and not excited about living in an isolated house that was a three-mile walk to school if I missed the bus. However, I made new friends readily enough, enjoyed my life and found it to be a wholesome environment. There was little crime, and I grew up with a sense of freedom and possibility. My classmates aspired to more than the ones I had left behind and I enjoyed decent relationships with most of my teachers.

I never really internalised this knowledge, but my teachers seemed to believe I had a lot of potential. My report cards always had some variant of 'could do better' or 'is just coasting along' and nothing changed now that I was in a new world. I was smart (I thought I was the smartest person in the room) and it must have been infuriating for the people charged with turning me into a productive member of society that I was such a waster. Unfortunately, I just didn't care and floated along without any real interest in achieving anything, largely unconcerned with nebulous concepts like 'the future'.

One day in my final year of school my computer science teacher, Mrs O'Grady, shared an interesting anecdote. She was on some kind of professional development course and had been set homework to write sample character evaluations of a few of her students. Her summary of me was that I was the kind of person who, in ten years, would either be running a successful business or else in prison!

Everyone in the class had a good laugh at this, especially as my future was already mapped out. I had developed a passion for aeroplanes and was on track to join the Royal Air Force as a fast jet pilot. I had passed all the aptitude tests easily and won a scholarship, and so – almost by default – my career path was already decided.

After I left school with shockingly bad exam results, the RAF insisted I complete a six-month officer training course at the RAF College in Cranwell, Lincolnshire, where I would learn to be a leader of men. This wasn't something I had ever thought about or had any interest in, and I didn't treat it with the seriousness they expected. I was there to fly. Just that. Instead of leaning in and committing fully to what I had signed up for, I treated it like a continuation of school, with predictable results: I failed the course and had to go figure out my future instead.

This was hard – my first real experience of failure. I had been going to join the Air Force for as long as people had been asking me what I was going to do with my life and now I was lost. Nobody knew what to tell me either, although one person did share a nugget of wisdom that has been with me ever since: no experience is wasted.

I never did get to fly aeroplanes for a living, but after travelling around Europe for a few months and doing various odd jobs after that, including a stint working in sales, I eventually found my feet and started a small business that did quite well for a while. Money was rolling in. I was travelling regularly and even talking about one day buying my own aeroplane if things carried on as they were.

Unfortunately, business is hard, especially if you haven't learned the lessons you've been given. I didn't have a proper handle on what I was doing and made some poor decisions. Gradually it all got out of control and I found myself running faster but not getting ahead. Money was coming in, but I was sinking into debt and working harder and harder to keep my head above water. I was making promises I couldn't keep to customers and was stuck, doing the same thing as I had always done, afraid to accept that it wasn't working.

Almost ten years after that conversation in high school it came back to haunt me. I stood in a courtroom being lectured about the things I needed to do within 30 days if I was to avoid going to prison. Boy, did it burn.

Calling it quits was hard to do but I had to acknowledge the reality I had been denying and give up the fight. And so, on my 28th birthday, after narrowly avoiding being sent to spend time at Her Majesty's pleasure, I left the UK to make a fresh start.

In many ways, it was the making of me. I had learned the value of hard work, the importance of getting your shit together and how to be more dispassionate in my decision-making. Along the way, I sacrificed a lot of relationships, made enemies and burned a lot of bridges. I had become a better person but at a great cost.

Now all I had in the world was £150 in my pocket and a rucksack. I was wiser, bloodied but still standing, and was mentally prepared for a fresh start somewhere where I didn't have a history and reputation. I put my second great failure behind me, as I had done with the first, and hitch-hiked to Germany to find a job on a building site.

In Germany, I adapted, I improvised and I overcame. This was the mid-1990s – the east of the country was rebuilding after decades of neglect under the communists and there were tens of thousands of British and Irish workers like me all looking for ways to make some money. I quickly found a job, then another, and started to build a network of people through work. I made an effort to learn the language and quickly found myself being pushed to the front of the crowd whenever there was any communicating to be done. I was in a position of leadership but unfortunately wasn't ready to lead.

It came to a head in one job where I was one of the first on-site and, as more and more people arrived over the following weeks, my role evolved from the boss asking me to 'tell these guys what paperwork they need' to 'show them around and tell them what's to be done' and ultimately to 'how many men can you spare to start on X?' and 'what's the status of Y, why is it taking so long?'

Without wanting it, I had become the manager of 30 or so construction workers. They were tough, direct, poorly educated people and far from home in precarious circumstances. They didn't speak the local language, most had been ripped off more than once and they were suspicious of this posh kid who was 'in with the Germans'. I was out of my depth just trying to administer the work and not thinking about the leadership aspect of it all. Once again it was threatening to spiral out of control. Fortunately, there was an intervention before I could screw up too badly.

I was doing my rounds, trying to schedule everyone's lunch breaks so that only a few were absent at a time when one fellow rebelled. He refused to let me tell him when he could take his break and I reared up in response, the two of us shouting and glaring at each other. Then, in a much quieter and plaintive voice, he said, 'You're treating these men like shit.'

That hurt and I was at a loss for words. We had known each other for a while, and I respected him, so he was able to tell me a plain truth: I was so focused on getting the job done that I had forgotten they were people.

I finally started applying what I had been taught about leadership by the RAF a decade before. I walked around the site talking to everyone individually. I apologised, discussed their needs and recognised that they were all trying to get the job done too. I asked for ideas and shook hands, and from then on, I focused on playing the role I had been landed with.

As I relaxed and started trusting people, managing the work suddenly got a lot easier. I still had to make decisions and assign work, but now I focused on empowering them to concentrate on what they were good at and spent my energy supporting them instead of trying to micro-manage their activities. I didn't become a great boss, far from it, but at least I had the basics under control and people started to have confidence in me. A week or so later, someone commented that

I seemed to be handling the job much better and that everyone was happier as a result. Lesson learned and internalised. Finally, I was starting to earn my position of authority!

I believe I was able to do this because I was consciously thinking about my role and what it was based on. I needed to be competent and up *to* the challenge, not just up *for* it. That lesson has become part of who I am today. Having internalised it two decades previously, I couldn't help measuring my CPL managers against the same standard I set myself: get the basics under control and don't treat people like shit.

Although I made money in Germany, as did many others, getting ripped off was an occupational hazard and a regular occurrence. Sometimes I had to go into a room full of stressed, angry construction workers and explain that nobody was getting paid. Many of them would spend their last pfennigs on beer while waiting for me to report back and there was always the danger that things could turn to violence. I had to be careful, tough and confident in order to take control and exercise authority effectively. After that experience, I never let anyone push me around again.

—

I stayed in Germany for three years and had a fantastic time. I worked an average of over 60 hours a week and consumed heroic quantities of fine German beer in my off time. However, an economic downturn was looming and I knew it would be important not to be stuck. It was time to do something different so I took what money I had saved and set off to work my way around the world, a decision that eventually brought me to Taiwan.

It was in Taiwan that I learned the lesson that is central to my understanding of Facebook's problem with how they manage their contractors. I had been in the country a few years and had a full roster of good gigs doing everything from corporate training to pre-MBA classes at language schools to private tutoring. Like everyone else in the same situation, I was having second thoughts. It becomes apparent to all of us eventually that our job is to do as we are told and if you get uppity you will quickly find yourself looking for a new one.

One of my teacher friends, who had yet to learn this, got into an argument with his boss at a high school. He felt that the emphasis on testing and rote-learning was counterproductive and, as a properly qualified teacher, he wanted to try more enlightened methods. He thought he was the smartest person in the room and just didn't get that he was working for a business with its own agenda. His concern with pedagogy was not aligned with the needs and objectives of the organisation that paid his wages.

When he threatened to resign, his boss replied, 'In Taiwan, we have a saying that foreign English teachers are like potatoes: they're all the same and if you need another one you just put your hand in the ground and pull one out.'

I had already more or less figured this out for myself, but having it stated so explicitly focused my mind on the fact that

I wasn't an expert partner: I was just a commodity. Unlike my friend, I didn't waste any energy getting upset about it. I applied some sales thinking and accepted that I needed to differentiate my brand so that I could be seen as adding more value and I could therefore have more control over my working conditions and make more money.

From then on I pursued a strategy of getting results, which was defined as having happy students who want to continue the class and pay more money. This was the only metric anyone cared about. Instead of trudging through boring textbooks, I engaged with my students on the topics they cared about. This was a lot more work for me but much more rewarding.

We talked about their professional activities, their plans, their issues and the stuff they needed to be able to manage in English, and the language learning thus became an organic part of a bigger project for them. It was edutainment, a mix of fun and learning that my students responded well to, and which worked for me as well.

You can imagine that my relationship with these students was complex. They were often not the ones paying for the classes and there might be a school manager or, worse, someone from HR, trying to control what was going on. Everyone had boxes that needed to be ticked, and of course, they were not education experts. They didn't know what was best, only what was the acknowledged way of doing things, and they expected us 'foreign experts' to follow orders.

Although they called us 'foreign experts' to our faces, we in the foreign-teacher community knew there was a different name for us, one which all of us heard in the wild eventually: white monkeys.

A white monkey is, generally speaking, a white foreigner in Taiwan who is hired to do a 'face job' (usually modelling, advertising or language teaching) based on the perception that association with white foreigners signifies legitimacy and prestige. White monkeys don't add a lot of value, they're a necessary evil to be tolerated in the business of teaching your customers to communicate the way you want them to. White monkeys are not skilled, they're there to do the repetitive grunt work, to grade the homework, and you can hire pretty much anyone to do the job if they speak the language. So long as you can show them to the world occasionally and say, 'Look, we have these people', who cares?

I successfully escaped the 'white monkey' label by thinking deeply about how to make myself more valuable and, in the autumn of 2017, I was trying to apply the same thinking to my work as a content moderator for Facebook. CPL made it abundantly clear to me on many occasions that my job was simply to do as I was told, to have no opinions, and it seemed to me that they had the same problem with their client as I used to have with mine in Taiwan.

Facebook was paying CPL to make a problem go away. CPL's role was defined for them by the client (Facebook), in the same way that my friend was told what and how to teach. Success and effectiveness were measured in terms of compliance with narrow goals set by administrators, rather than by looking at the big picture: are the people using your service happy, and how are you, as a contractor or freelancer, contributing to that?

It was a shit show of the first order and not because anyone was a bad person or the people at the top were incompetent at writing policy and didn't care about anyone's well-being. All the issues that were appearing were created by a dysfunctional system. Very few people could recognise this, and even when they did, they were unable to change the way the system worked. When Pedro tried to tinker with one small part of it, all that achieved was to send the whole project off the rails for a while.

I'm getting ahead of myself. Before returning to the story, there's one piece of the puzzle still missing that will allow us to understand why otherwise rational people had allowed this state of affairs to come into being.

—

In 1829 the British Parliament passed the Metropolitan Police Act, which established a force (now known as a service) that functioned on the premise of 'policing by consent'. The idea was that for the public to have confidence in the police, they had to be seen to be impartial and fair, accountable, representative of the population and to always use the minimum of force required.

Ireland's modern police force works on the same principle and is known as An Garda Síochána, which translates as 'the guardians of the peace'. Like their British counterparts, they are unarmed and trained to de-escalate conflict, engage with the public and obtain a commitment to lawful behaviour without resorting to violence.

In practice, it's a far from perfect system, but it works well enough. For example, during the Covid-19 lockdowns, the Irish parliament considered giving the Gardaí increased powers to enter people's homes and put a stop to private parties, which were prohibited under the emergency health regulations. The Gardaí pushed back against being given additional powers, on the grounds that this would harm the relationship with the general public and ultimately reduce their moral authority and effectiveness.

In contrast, the emphasis in the United States is on enforcement (the use of force to make people follow rules), not on engaging with them so that they voluntarily change their behaviour. The police are heavily armed, increasingly indistinguishable from a paramilitary force and focused on obtaining compliance rather than commitment.

As an American organisation, Facebook has a content moderation strategy that relies on obtaining compliance instead of earning commitment. Everything works on the basis that the company has the power to decide what's okay and will use that power without hesitation. There is no mechanism for the user to build a relationship with that power, to be heard and respected.

While I'm not sure how you would build a relationship with two billion people who have wildly differing opinions about pretty much everything, I haven't seen any evidence that Facebook has ever even considered it. There is no conversation about how to lead the public to accept a code of conduct that nobody fully agrees with but which serves the needs of all of us well enough that the sacrifice is worthwhile.

Generally speaking, we agree to follow the rules of civilisation because we want society to function successfully, not because we're afraid of getting caught breaking those rules. As long as we have confidence in the framework in general, even if we disagree with some parts of it, we learn to work with it.

A lot of the debate around content moderation boils down to a lack of confidence in the objectives and the fairness of the existing system. There is no trust, because power is being wielded without accountability or transparency, no leadership from the people with the power and no messaging that this is a shared endeavour and that we have to figure it out together.

The only message is that Facebook is the only authority, the only one who can find a solution, and everyone else just has to do what they are told. This command and control mentality, justified by the belief that 'we're the smartest people in the room', makes it impossible for Facebook to receive and act on genuine feedback about how well their systems are working. Reports are sanitised, the wrong numbers are emphasised and managers are incentivised to protect themselves at the expense of truth.

That's why my simple chat with Pedro at the end of the last chapter set in motion a whole series of events that ultimately put me in an untenable position. It's going to take a few chapters to tell, so let's go back to my first experiences working with the day shift after the NGO had finally concluded.

SEVEN

WHEN ALL ELSE FAILS

After working my first weekend shift with the daytime team, I had a day off on the Monday. One of my colleagues phoned me late that evening, He was quite nervous and asked me not to shoot the messenger, but the team had elected him to give me some bad news. Apparently, the senior management had called Eve10 into a 'last chance' team meeting and told them that everyone was required to move to the day shift until their quality scores improved. Anyone not reaching the required standard would be fired.

It all smelled of panic, again. We were a problem that nobody knew how to fix and some garbled version of my explanation had prompted this over-the-top solution from people who didn't know what they were doing. The call centre mentality was getting in the way of getting the job done.

Despite my friend's concern, I was fairly relaxed about the whole thing. I felt vindicated and was confident the result would be a rapid improvement in quality scores. If the scores started to drop again when we resumed our regular shift, that would confirm my theory. The only fly in the ointment was that we were being asked to disrupt our sleep schedule and take a pretty hefty pay cut because we were losing the extra allowances we got for working evenings. It seemed like an acceptable sacrifice for a week, so I showed up the next morning feeling quite positive.

Of course, I was thinking like a normal human being and had forgotten that I was working for CPL, an organisation that only excelled at management screw-ups.

We arrived to find that there were no workstations for us. We were not good enough to be trusted to do the work any more, so instead we were treated like newbies and ordered to shadow the daytime staff. This caused a lot of disruption for them, so their productivity dropped at the same time as they took responsibility for doing all the work we would usually do in the evenings. It was a complete disaster and by the second day the entire evening team was sitting in a corner twiddling our thumbs while the day shift tried to cope with the backlog of tickets.

TL Damien was not with us – in fact, I never saw him again. He vanished from his desk and his name was never mentioned. He just ceased to exist, without fixing the numbers on my previous review. Instead, we reported to the day shift TL and also to Bill, of the NGO fame, who came wandering by from time to time. I don't know what his other job was or even exactly what the proper chain of command was. It was all very confusing, and where there is confusion there are complaints and defensiveness.

I was strolling unenthusiastically back from the bathroom to the corner where we were supposed to be revising policy or some such when I bumped into Bill, who gave me a faux cheerful greeting and asked me how I was doing. So I told him. I was bored, wasting my time and annoyed at being forced to take a pay cut. I asked when we would be able to go back to work.

He didn't like this one bit and snapped that I needed to respect the needs and objectives of the organisation. I replied that to pay me to sit and do nothing wasn't contributing to the bottom line and that the organisation needed me to be at work fulfilling their objectives. I think there might have been a follow-up exchange about available resources, which highlighted to me that he believed we were the problem, not that management is responsible when 20 people are allegedly failing. Then I walked away from him, or he walked away from me, I don't remember which.

It wasn't long before I was pulled into a meeting room with my two temporary TLs and told that they didn't like my attitude. They wanted to make it very clear to me that I was required to be there with the day shift no matter how much I objected. They genuinely thought I simply resented the change. I tried to explain that it had been my idea, I was all for it and everyone just wanted to get to work, but they didn't want to hear it.

The problem was that they were low-level managers who had been ordered to implement a solution that nobody had thought through. They just didn't know what to do with us, and the CPL way is to stomp on criticism rather than acknowledge problems. Their client, Facebook, set the tone with their mentality, and my employers embraced it wholeheartedly to the point that any critical thought was perceived as a threat.

I was trying to find a solution, a way forward, and tried to establish a little credibility by telling them that I had 15 years' experience designing and delivering training courses for adults. I didn't get as far as making suggestions for how we could make do with limited resources to get better results because Bill cut me off with 'Nobody cares what experience you have. Your job is to do as you're told. You go where we tell you, do the work we assign to you, keep your opinions to yourself, and if you can't reach the required standard with the available resources, then you have no future with this organisation.'

That was that, sort of. We kept our heads down and, a few days later, they randomly decided to let us work alongside the day shift. Although we hadn't passed any defined milestone, our quality scores eventually improved. We hung on through most of December right up to Christmas with the day shift and then we were deemed good enough to go back to the evening work on our own – without even a TL to keep an eye on us! However, all of the auditors were still drawn from the day shift and there was no real plan for ongoing synchronisation, so the structural problem remained unsolved and the quality issues began to reappear in the new year.

It was all very well for me to complain that Eve10's time was being wasted, but the whole situation was also terribly unfair to the regular daytime shift. They had work to do and targets to meet. They were already overworked before we descended upon them like a bunch of lost children needing babysitting.

The auditors had the worst of it. The evening shift couldn't share the auditing workload and we had been instructed by our TL to appeal every auditing decision we thought we could possibly win in order to improve our quality scores. When our auditing appeals were processed properly, we won back three out of four of them – and that's a big deal when you're only allowed to make four or five mistakes a month – but there was a huge backlog of appeals they didn't have time to deal with and the rule was that they had to be processed within two weeks of the original audit. Anything that wasn't dealt with within this time became permanent. A lot of my appeals over the previous couple of months had failed because the auditors hadn't got around to dealing with them in time.

I blamed the system, not the individuals, but was increasingly frustrated that my quality score was lower than it needed to be simply because nobody had time to look and say, 'Oh yes, that girl is a famous model in her own country even though none of us here have heard of her, so she's classed as a public figure and not protected by the bullying policy after all'.

There was a lot of bad feeling among the evening team about this. There's no point complaining to people about their quality scores if they're not being given the opportunity to justify the decisions they've made. This issue eventually came to a head in a team meeting.

We had all been invited to share examples of 'problematic' content, so I produced my backlog of unanswered appeals, and the guy in charge of the room agreed with me on about three-quarters of them. I told him pretty directly that if the auditors would just do their jobs then the supposed quality problem would get a lot smaller. I explained that I wasn't going to waste any more time appealing audit decisions, because nobody was reviewing them.

He was horrified and didn't seem to grasp that it wasn't a case of my not wanting to work with the system: it was that the system wasn't working. 'But you will be put on a PIP (personal improvement plan)!' he replied in a shocked voice.

I paused. I hadn't considered this. I was just being bolshy, but I suddenly realised that the very first thing they do when putting somebody on a PIP is to review the mistakes they've made, and the way forward was suddenly very clear.

'If I'm on a PIP,' I replied, 'they would have to go back and acknowledge that a lot of my so-called mistakes were correct decisions. With those auditing decisions corrected, it would be clear that my quality score was a lot better than I had been given credit for, and I was only on the PIP because my appeals had not been processed in time.'

This was all off the cuff but started to make a lot of sense as I said it. He went running off to talk to the auditors in a panic and within 30 minutes my backlog of appeals had been cleared! Unfortunately, a lot of them were outside the two-week limit and my quality score from the previous month could not be adjusted retrospectively. Many of them dated back to the NGO. In fact, the only reason I had so many mistakes to appeal in the first place was that I had been working more tickets than normal and had been audited more heavily than all the people whose quiz scores were not as high as mine because my managers had been focused on the wrong things.

Still, after months of asking nicely and getting nowhere, I had managed to force a resolution and our audit appeals were now being dealt with promptly. I'm sure I pissed a few people off, but I make no apologies for it. Teamwork does not mean letting yourself be penalised for systemic failures, or anyone else's laziness, and our quality scores as a team suddenly got a lot better, so I consider it a win.

—

It was around this time that I had a further interaction with the counsellors. Just before we started working daytimes, resilience training was organised for some team members. This mainly comprised sitting around a conference table and doing some deep breathing to get in touch with our emotions. Everyone was a bit uncomfortable. Although we went through the motions, we were all relieved to go back to our desks and fill in the feedback form saying how helpful it all was.

I couldn't bring myself to play the game any longer and instead told them I needed help. I wrote on the form that I had realised I felt overwhelmed and had lost my confidence. However, that statement didn't do justice to my state of mind that evening. I remember sitting at my desk, staring at the screen blankly when it came time to do the work, not knowing what to do.

I was paralysed with indecision, on the edge of panic. I sent a quick message to my colleague from the NGO, the 'just protecting my quality by doing the minimum of hi-pri work' guy, who was sitting a few seats away, and then stumbled over to the canteen area with about as much self-awareness as a jilted lover walking away from a breakup. I was a mess. I remember sitting at the table with my friend and telling him I felt completely lost and didn't know what I was doing. Nothing made any sense and I felt like nothing I did would make any difference.

I remember hitch-hiking across Germany without a map as a teenager. I remember digging my car out of the sand after getting bogged on a remote beach in Australia, in a frantic race against a rising tide. I remember visiting the Taj Mahal while the whole city was under martial law and having the place all to myself. In each of these situations I had agency, I had the power to cope, to do something, to decide the outcome, to deal with whatever the world might throw at me.

Now I was trapped in a shitty corporate job, and I was as powerless as everyone else working in crappy offices with crappy bosses. I was also starting to realise that I was simultaneously being exposed to massive quantities of toxic material.

I have barely mentioned the specifics of my daily bread and butter as a content moderator. If you want to read the gory details you can find them in the afterword at the end of the book. Let's just say at this point that if you're arguing with your auditors about whether a baby is dead, and the only thing that matters is winning the argument so you can improve your quality score, then that's probably a bit dehumanising. Nobody cares about the baby any more, we're not superheroes there to protect the innocent; we're just corporate drones focused on making the numbers.

We were being relentlessly bombarded with images of death and destruction, reading hateful and spiteful comments, adjudicating petty squabbles between small-minded people, seeing cheerful kids with disabilities being electrocuted in the genitals by some maniac with a mosquito zapper, 100 tickets an hour, all day every day. We never had time to process and compartmentalise what we were seeing; we just had to make quick decisions and move on.

It seems obvious to me now that this would have an impact – that the cumulative effects of this would be harmful to at least some of us – but at the time I didn't know what was going on. Everything came to a head for me that evening. I guess the wellness team should take the credit – or the blame – for making it happen. That session made me aware of the pressure that had been building for months. I asked for help. I asked for one-to-one counselling because I was feeling overwhelmed.

It took two weeks for them to schedule an appointment (by which time I was enmeshed in the debacle with the day team). To this day I have no memory of that counselling session. All I remember is that I came away convinced I had wasted my time and that they couldn't help me. Certainly, nothing changed in our working conditions. In fact, things went from bad to worse at around this time.

EIGHT

GUILTY UNTIL PROVEN INNOCENT

Let's rewind the clock a bit to talk about Maria, whose story starts way back in September 2017 at about the same time the evening shift guys were being organised into market teams.

Maria was from an immigrant background, worked on the day shift and, coinciding with the move to the Beckett building, joined a new team called Ground Truth. This was a big change for her because up to this point she had been doing GI work, also known as access and authenticity.

By the end of September, with the support of TL Damien, I had made three requests in writing for additional GI training, but so far nothing had happened. This came to a head when my GI auditor found a quality mistake, which I appealed on the grounds that the correct action for that case was not written down anywhere. She replied that I was supposed to know how to do my job, I replied that I had made multiple requests for the training I needed to do my job, and so on and so on.

By now you can probably guess how that played out. The auditor was also the trainer that I had asked for help, and there was no way she was going to admit that I didn't know how to do my job, because she hadn't done hers. I won't go into any more detail, but you'll see later that this is relevant to Maria's story.

One day in early October, Maria's new TL came rushing over to her in a bit of a panic. Both of them were required to go to a conference room to assist with an investigation with just 15 minutes' notice. Neither of them had any idea what was going on, or any chance to prepare. They were the only people in the room, and they were joined via video link by an investigator from Facebook who, without giving any explanation, started to question Maria. She wanted to know about her actions with regard to one specific user a month previously, back when she had been doing GI.

Maria typically handled over 1,000 tickets a day in that role and didn't remember any of them. Why would she? The job is to process the ticket and then give your full attention to the next one. She was completely taken aback and didn't have any answers.

Within 15 minutes the investigation was over and both of them left the room not sure what had just happened. They found out soon enough when, a few days later, Maria was suspended from work pending the outcome of an investigation by CPL into some unspecified gross misconduct, which is grounds for instant dismissal without notice.

She was escorted from the building by security, without being given any clear explanation of what the allegations were.

They took her ID badge and she found herself standing on the street outside in a bit of a daze. She looked around to see one of her colleagues from her old team sitting despondently on a wall nearby. It turned out that the same thing had just happened to her. Both of them had just been disappeared from their desks and would never be mentioned again by their colleagues. They would just cease to exist.

I didn't know anything about this until my wife asked me to give Maria some advice a week later. They had become good friends over the last year. One of the disadvantages of being older and more experienced is that people who need help tend to look at you and say, 'That guy probably knows what he's doing, I'll ask him.' I found myself agreeing to accompany her to the investigation hearing the following week.

We sat down for a chat first so I could try and get my head around what was going on. It was a mess. Maria was very stressed, and I had trouble getting the full story, but as far as I could tell the situation was as follows:

On the day in question, a month previously, it was alleged by Facebook that Maria and her colleague had both taken an unhealthy interest in a specific user even though neither of them was working a ticket relating to them. It was claimed that they had both accessed the user control panel (UCP), which holds information about user identities and contact details. Access to the UCP is restricted and only permitted with good reason.

They also claimed that Maria had searched for the user's profile from her own personal Facebook account and had sent a friend request to them several years before but then cancelled it.

The stuff about her private Facebook account shocked me. It suggested that Facebook was monitoring the private accounts of their contractors and looking for evidence of wrongdoing. This was the incident that made me go and look at my own contract and realise that we had been suckered into giving Facebook the right to collect data and monitor our private communications on their platform. As such, Facebook could use information from Maria's private Facebook account against her.

The claim about misuse of the UCP seemed pretty cut and dried. There are situations where you might need to access the UCP as part of normal GI work – in fact, I even dug up records of chat conversations about the UCP I had had with TLs and trainers while trying to make sense of the workflows, but if there isn't a ticket corresponding to that user, well, that looked like a privacy violation and it seemed that Facebook had now handed responsibility for dealing with it to CPL.

Interestingly, on the same day that these two people were suspended from work after allegedly breaking the rules on user privacy, every team in the building was given a refresher training on that exact topic. Taking everyone off-task for an hour is expensive and not something a sane employer would do in response to an isolated incident. You would only do that if you thought you had some kind of systemic or training problem that needed to be fixed, right?

I couldn't give Maria a lot of advice except to focus on procedural stuff. She was being called into a disciplinary hearing but hadn't been formally notified of the charges against her. It seemed like it was up to her to figure out what they thought she had done wrong by analysing the questions they had asked in the previous meeting. That put her in an unfair situation, so I told her to start the meeting by protesting that she had not been given a chance to prepare a defence.

The only other lifeline I could think of was the legal principle of the presumption of innocence. If anyone wants to accuse an employee of wrongdoing, it's up to them to prove their claim. You can't just make an accusation and require the employee to disprove it.

If your employer takes your ID badge and evicts you from the building, it's highly likely that you're never going back so there's no point trying to appease them when they go through the motions of a disciplinary hearing. It looked to me as if Facebook had uncovered something – maybe through illegal means – that seemed at first glance to be a violation of their rules around user privacy, and they were not going to give it a second look. I guessed they had told CPL they didn't want that person in the building any more and now CPL needed to find a justification for firing her. All you can do in that situation is make it difficult for them while still preparing for the worst.

If Maria could refuse to go quietly on the grounds that the disciplinary hearing was improperly conducted, she could drag the process out and keep on getting paid while she looked for another job. That was the best-case scenario.

CPL's rules for disciplinary procedures allow the accused to bring a colleague to support them, and Maria chose me. I wasn't allowed to speak, which seemed grossly unfair given that she was facing two people: a TL conducting the investigation and someone from HR to take notes, both senior to her and both familiar with the procedures and cultural/legal background to what was going on.

On the other hand, I had my phone in my pocket and activated the voice recorder before going in. I made notes as well, writing down my objections and questions about what was going on. The investigators made life easier for us by assuming they could just go through the motions. They hadn't prepared properly and didn't know how to respond when Maria took control of the meeting at the start by objecting that she hadn't been given any explanation or information in advance of the meeting.

All they could do was note her objection and press on with their very simple line of inquiry: why did you take this action on this user account on this date? Maria's simple reply to that was that she worked over 1,000 tickets a day and had no memory of the alleged incident. She couldn't give any explanation and didn't even accept the claims being made. Then she asked for proof.

That should have brought the meeting to a close. The TL was floundering, but then the HR rep decided to get involved and asked if it was possible that someone else had accessed the secure internal network using Maria's computer. I had to bite my tongue to keep quiet but was delighted by this. Not only was she speculating inappropriately but I still had the bitter memory of getting told off for drawing attention to exactly this kind of 'fraping'.

Maria knew about my experience, so she told Laurel and Hardy that fraping was a common occurrence. The HR rep replied in shock, 'But that's a fireable offence! Why haven't you ever reported it?'

The TL kept very quiet while Maria explained that she knew somebody who had once tried to report it and was still dealing with the consequences of rocking the boat. The HR rep quickly changed tack. She spent maybe another 30 minutes digging and asking questions, trying to get an admission of guilt from Maria, who stuck to her guns. She didn't know what they were talking about and it was up to them to provide evidence if they wanted to accuse her of anything. That was all she was going to say.

I was really satisfied with how the meeting had gone. I had taken an instant dislike to both Laurel and Hardy because of their presumptive attitude and took great pleasure in seeing them floundering when things didn't go as they expected. I had learned a lot more about the details of the alleged incident from their questions and was confident we could put together a good defence for the next round.

—

The HR rep was supposed to send a copy of the meeting notes and, after waiting a few days, we started sending emails to request them. It took a week to get them and the first thing I did after receiving the Word file she sent was look to see when it had been created. Yup, she had been too busy asking questions – which was not her job – to take notes on the day and had only got around to creating our copy of the meeting notes the night before sending them to us. Things were just getting better and better.

I went through the document she sent quite forensically, comparing it to the recording I had made and then sent it back with a very long list of objections. Then we had to have another meeting to clarify what was said in the first meeting and agree on what the official record should say. That meeting took much longer than the original investigative meeting and we ran out of time before we reached the end of the list.

This was in CPL's office building, not Beckett, and they evicted us from the room at 6 p.m. because they wanted to lock the doors and turn the lights out. It was a farce and would have been great fun except that on the way in we met Maria's co-accused. She hadn't talked to me and she was there for her outcome meeting – the outcome being that CPL fired her for gross misconduct without any paid notice.

I had to share a taxi back to the Beckett Building with the HR rep and her boss. This was quite uncomfortable, as you can imagine. It was also the evening rush hour and took forever, so I was an hour late starting my work and my TL needed authorisation from HR not to penalise me.

I sent an email to HR, thinking nothing of it, and received a very sniffy reply from 'Sharon' letting me know that they didn't like my signature line. I was using an image that had come up in the queues one day depicting a 'Facebook police' car with the caption *Shit, here come the cops, don't say anything funny!* Okay, it wasn't very professional, but I never had cause to email anyone except for my team, and my TL had never objected. Unfortunately, now HR had seen it and I was getting told off! I removed it immediately, sent an apology and forgot about it – for the time being.

Eventually, Maria was called in for her outcome meeting, and I came along too. The outcome of the investigation was that Maria had not been given a fair opportunity to defend herself, and therefore there would be a new investigation, to be conducted by different people. In plain English: 'we screwed this up and can't get away with firing you just yet so we're going to try again'.

—

The next investigation meeting hearing a week or so later was a much more professional affair. I heard from a senior TL after the dust settled that we had prompted internal reforms to the way they handle these things, with a focus on increased professionalism. They tried to do everything by the book, but old habits die hard and Sharon from HR – she who had recently objected to my signature line – couldn't help expressing opinions and arguing a couple of times when she was supposed to be just taking notes. She was fixated on one interpretation of events and was going to pursue it to the exclusion of any other.

As before, I had primed Maria to take control of the proceedings from the start. They explained what she was accused of and were ready to start with the questions. However, I had worked out that they were asking the wrong questions, and letting them decide what was important was not a winning strategy. We needed to take control, so Maria ignored the first question and explained that, because she struggled with English sometimes, she had prepared a statement that she wanted to read first.

Sharon from HR tried to prevent her from reading it, but Maria fought her corner and argued that the only reason we were having this second investigation was that she hadn't been allowed to have her say the first time around. Sharon had no choice and eventually acquiesced, partly because the investigating TL was happy to hear what she wanted to say. He seemed to be taking the responsibility seriously and his conduct throughout the investigation was beyond reproach.

Maria's statement started by talking about the Costa Concordia cruise liner, which had run aground a short time earlier and sank with the loss of 32 lives and at a cost of billions of dollars. The captain of the ship, and company executives, tried to place all of the blame on the poor schmuck who was holding the wheel at the time of the accident but the official inquiry had ruled that this guy was simply doing what he had been ordered to do and was not trained or empowered to dispute the decisions of his superiors.

The investigation ruled that the captain was to blame, even though – in fact, because – he was in his cabin at the time of the incident. He was responsible for putting the wrong person in the wrong position, for not knowing what was going on in his organisation and for creating a culture that allowed his team to ignore best practices and cut corners with disastrous results. The company's crisis director, who had not even been on the ship, was sentenced to nearly three years' prison time as punishment for trying to hide the truth about what had happened and blame the little guy.

The message to CPL was unequivocal: you don't blame one individual for their mistakes if they're working within a system. You blame the systemic failures, and the people further up who perpetuate them.

In the first investigation meeting, I had learned the name of the user whose privacy had allegedly been violated. A quick Google search revealed several Facebook accounts in that name; all of them had been created at about the same time and had the same profile picture and basic biographical information. This was not just some random individual: this was suspicious activity of the sort that Maria and her team investigated every day. That's what they were there for.

While it appeared that Maria hadn't been officially investigating any report related to this user, and neither had her colleague who had already been fired, it seemed probable that somebody had.

Here's a little personal anecdote to shed some light on this. One evening one of my colleagues called out that the ticket he was working included a photo of a group of people, and one of them was somebody he knew. There is a rule that we're not allowed to work any tickets involving our friends, so he wanted someone else to take the ticket. I did it and thought nothing of it until I remembered that the rule also covered friends of friends as well.

I was friends with my colleague and had just worked a ticket related to one of his friends, so technically I had just broken the rules. But how would anybody know? In fact, how would I ever know if one of my tickets involved a friend of a friend?

Think about this. If you're Irish and have a normal number of friends on Facebook, say 400, and they all have a normal number of friends, that's 160,000 people, about 4 per cent of the number of people using Facebook in Ireland. Logically, 4 per cent of all the Irish content you see is going to involve one of these people, which is 20 or 30 tickets every night!

We were working the combined UK and Ireland queue, so the total number of users was much higher, but you get the idea. Sooner or later, all of us could expect to see content that we weren't allowed to work. Is it reasonable to expect us to recognise all of those 160,000 people every time?

Of course, it isn't, and in Maria's case, it was even more unreasonable. She had thousands of Facebook friends and didn't even know who most of them were. If each of them had an average number of friends as well, Maria's friends-of-friends list was probably more than a million people. There was no way she could be expected to recognise them all.

If you don't want your staff inadvertently breaking your rules, you need to program your system so that it doesn't give them any tickets they're not allowed to work. To the best of my knowledge, this is what Facebook does. The only time we saw content we were not allowed to work was when we recognised a face in an image. It never happened if their username was there, so I'm pretty sure some system was checking our friend connections before assigning tickets.

After I got involved with Maria's case I wondered if there was an official process we were supposed to follow in situations where we realised we had a connection to a ticket that the system had missed. I searched the various resources and reference documents but couldn't find anything, which is hardly surprising. If you're writing the rules and creating the systems, you can't anticipate every situation in advance. You're reliant on the people who do the work to come back to you and tell you what problems they're experiencing. However, the command and control, please-the-client-at-all-costs relationship meant that this feedback was never sent. Teams just figured out for themselves how they would handle new situations, and these informal solutions became unwritten standard procedures that everyone was supposed to know.

You may recall I described having a run-in with an auditor who insisted that I should know what to do even though I was arguing that there was no official document telling me. My problem was that because the evening shift was cut off from the institutional knowledge of the day shift, I couldn't learn the unofficial procedures from the people around me. Maria's problem was that she had learned procedures from the people around her that were not officially sanctioned by Facebook and Facebook was now assuming she had done something wrong.

I knew from my GI training that there were times when you might access the UCP to investigate suspicious accounts. When you use Facebook it places a small file called the DATR cookie on your device to track your activities, partly so they can target advertising at you but also for security. I was aware of scenarios – officially sanctioned – where you might access this data and learn that the same device was being used to manage multiple Facebook accounts and then investigate each one in turn to see if there was anything suspicious happening. In some markets, it's common for people to have multiple Facebook accounts: one for family and friends, one for work colleagues and another for chasing girls, for example. It's against Facebook's terms of service, but the users don't know that, so they use the same phone until they get caught out.

In that instance, you could get a ticket relating to one account, discover that there were a whole bunch of related accounts and then go and investigate those, without ever having a ticket for any of those accounts. I've done this and I've had conversations on chat with TLs and trainers about how to do it. It seemed perfectly reasonable to me that if a CM is presented with multiple accounts, all with the same name, they might find themselves investigating all of them even though they only had a ticket corresponding to one of them.

If Facebook had wanted to know what was going on in Maria's case, they could have done the process in reverse. It would be pretty easy to say, 'Maria and her colleague both looked at the UCP for user X; let's see if there were any other accounts being managed from the same device and check whether any of those had been reported for any reason.' This didn't happen, and if I had tried to do that research without authorisation, I would have found myself getting fired.

Sometimes when you're following these investigative trails, the system will block you because of the rule about working on friends' accounts. You may not know user X, the one you're investigating, but if you discover they also have an account as user Y, and user Y is a scam artist who has made friends with as many people as possible, including one of your friends, then the system will prevent you from investigating them.

This seems like the right thing to do, but what do you do if you've just spent 20 minutes investigating all the different accounts this guy is running and now the system is blocking you? You're being managed by the numbers, you have productivity targets to meet and maybe you haven't fully thought through what the rules mean. Would you just ask one of your colleagues to deal with it? It certainly seems like the easiest solution to the problem.

Maria told me that this happened all the time on her team. A colleague asks you to look something up for them and you help out without ever wondering how the client might feel about that. Everyone is doing it; you only get a couple of weeks of formal training and Facebook executives are on record as saying that most training is on the job. Of course, you're just going to accept the procedures that everybody else is following. Maria told me she would be blocked by the system every few days because she had so many friends-of-friends and thought that asking her colleagues to help her was the officially approved way of getting the job done.

I looked in the reference manuals, and there was no mention of what to do in this situation. It was something Facebook had just never thought of, and teams had found their own workarounds for it. Maria had been at CPL / Facebook for a long time and had had three different TLs in that time, none of whom had ever raised any concerns at hearing their team ask each other out loud to help them bypass the security restrictions. It was like the culture of fraping – a failure of management to think properly about what they were doing.

Maria's statement outlined a couple of different scenarios in which CMs might be legitimately looking at a user's confidential data without a corresponding ticket. She pointed out that if two people on the same team are investigating the same user on the same day, and the user clearly has duplicate accounts, then there's probably something going on that needs to be properly investigated before you can say the CM did something they shouldn't have.

She also raised the question of cultural issues and how the values and assumptions that are taken for granted in one culture may be quite different from those in another. She quoted from Malcolm Gladwell's book *Outliers*, which describes numerous air disasters caused by poor communication as a result of an unhealthy power relationship – where people who saw themselves as junior failed to communicate some urgent piece of information because they were afraid of challenging authority.

Maria was from one of the Asian teams, and Asian cultures generally do not place the same emphasis on individual privacy as the West. The CPL way, dictated to them by Facebook, was to assume that everyone was a Silicon Valley engineer and had the same values and ways of doing things. I don't think it ever crossed their mind that the beliefs and behaviours they take for granted may not be universally shared. This is kind of ironic since the main reason we need content moderation is that the world is a wonderfully diverse place full of people with different perspectives and ideas.

After hearing all this, Sharon from HR wanted a paper copy, which we had prepared. We also put the original into an envelope and had her sign her name across the seal so there could be no dispute afterwards about what Maria had told them. Then the investigating TL worked through the list of questions that he had prepared in advance.

It was all much the same as the previous time around, except that Maria's answers usually started with 'As I just told you ...' They were trying to be very focused and to pin her down. This TL had done his homework and knew what he was doing, but now Maria was angry and defiant. She didn't want to satisfy them: she wanted them to acknowledge that they had put her in an impossible situation and that the fault was theirs.

I don't remember all of the details of the encounter (I had bottled out of recording it) but I do remember something interesting at the end. Sharon from HR was talking a lot, fixated on her own narrative, but the investigating TL wasn't listening to her. He was looking through Maria's statement and reading parts of it with extreme interest. When he put the papers down he made that shape with his mouth that people make when they reluctantly agree with something and nodded.

A week later we were informed in the outcome meeting that there was to be another investigation. No explanation was given but the TL seemed quite uncomfortable. It seemed to me that he had accepted the argument we had made and was not willing to find Maria guilty of gross misconduct, but Sharon from HR needed to fire her. The only way out for her was to do the whole thing again and find a more compliant TL who would act in the company's interest instead of being fair.

So we did it all again over the next couple of weeks. I won't bore you with the details, except to say that Sharon from HR stopped trying to maintain the facade of fairness and professionalism. Fortunately, she had picked another intelligent and principled TL who reached the same conclusion as the previous one. And so the outcome was that there was to be yet another investigation – investigation number five.

In the meantime, Maria was still getting paid while she looked for other jobs. She had been offered a position working for another outside agency doing some other contract work for Facebook. She had been quite careful in what she had told them and hadn't actively misled them, but obviously the NDA prevented her from discussing any ongoing investigations or other confidential matters. I encouraged her to keep dragging out the process with CPL anyway, as there's no harm in getting paid twice or in making people squirm over their failures. That turned out to be a smart move.

On her first day at her new job, there was some confusion with the onboarding process. They didn't have a computer ready for her but she was still allowed into the building – GC4 this time, not Beckett. However, in the middle of the second day, two security guards appeared out of nowhere and escorted her apologetically out of the building without an explanation. The agency was trying frantically to find out what was going on and, after some back and forth, eventually informed Maria that Facebook had her listed as 'terminated permanently'. They were pretty angry but conceded Maria was not at fault, and now we had proof in writing: Facebook had ordered CPL to get rid of Maria without waiting for the outcome of their investigation, and now CPL were struggling to find an excuse to fire her.

By now it was the week before Christmas, the end of Eve10's purgatory on the day shift. Quality scores were up, morale was high and everybody was friends with everybody else at last. I was looking forward to earning lots of overtime over Christmas and taking a holiday in January. However, late on Tuesday afternoon, I got an email calling me to my six-month review, which was to be held in just 15 minutes. All of my pals who had joined at the same time as me got notifications giving them one or two days' notice, but I had to drop everything and go to a conference room straight away to be given the shitty news. They were extending my probation, which was supposed to be coming to an end that day because of my alleged disruptive behaviour and bad attitude.

They repeated what Bill had said a couple of weeks earlier but wouldn't even listen when I asked if I was allowed to tell my side of the story. The decision was already made and was being relayed to me by two people I had never met before. Bill had disappeared, never to be seen again, and the day shift TL was off sick, so two random people had called me in at short notice. It didn't seem like a genuine review. I continued to protest and one of these two strangers got a bit rattled. She said that there were other reasons that hadn't been listed on the review documents and that HR had mentioned my signature line. At that point, everything became clear.

These kinds of reviews were supposed to be low-level management tasks. HR should not normally be involved with the day-to-day management of teams, but clearly Sharon from HR had talked to these people and I was sure it was no coincidence that Maria's next investigation meeting was scheduled for the following morning. I was being warned off. They wanted me out of the picture so Maria would have to fight her corner on her own.

It wasn't necessary: we knew what was coming and there didn't seem much point fighting it any longer. Better to let CPL do the dirty deed and put in a pro forma appeal, and after it was rejected, Maria would be free to make a claim against them for unfair dismissal. However, I had stupidly drawn attention to myself and now I was in their cross hairs too.

Maria went to the meeting the next morning alone and without the prepared statement. She refused to answer any questions because she had already been investigated four times and didn't have anything more to add beyond what was in the statement she had already submitted twice. The investigating TL told her he hadn't seen that statement and requested a copy, so she promised to send it on and went home. But she didn't send it that afternoon: she waited 24 hours, emailing it to them around lunchtime on the Thursday, just one day before everyone went home for Christmas.

Two hours later, Sharon from HR called Maria and asked her to come to the outcome meeting the following morning. They had received her ten-page statement, considered all the points it raised, fully investigated the credible explanations she had given and were already confident in their conclusions. Maria declined the invitation, citing the employee handbook, which specified that they had to give her 24 hours' notice before calling her in for any meeting.

She also had holiday time scheduled over the Christmas break, which had been approved months before, so she ended up staying on salary until early January, instead of letting them run her out the door when it suited them. She was still unceremoniously fired at the beginning of January, on the grounds that she hadn't disproven their claims of gross misconduct; but, by fighting her corner, she had won herself more than two months of paid leave, whereas her colleague had been fired in a matter of days.

Maria immediately appealed on the basis that CPL had not conducted a fair investigation, claiming they had ignored her defence and repeated the process over and over until they got the outcome they wanted. She told them it was up to them to prove wrongdoing, which they had failed to do. As you can guess, this appeal was rejected by the site manager – who happened to be the sister of the TL who had fired her – because Maria had failed to prove that she was innocent.

—

Months later, after I had left CPL myself, I offered to help Maria bring a case for unfair dismissal to the WRC (the Workplace Relations Council), a state body that exists to provide a relatively quick and simple route for aggrieved employees to get justice.

It was a fairly simple procedure: you download a PDF

document from their website and fill it in, then just wait to see what happens. It took them a few months to respond but eventually one day my phone rang and it was a case officer wanting to know more about what had happened. I was in my new job as a tour guide by then, taking a bus full of people around the west of Ireland, but we talked through everything and a few weeks later they called me back to say that CPL wanted to settle the claim.

The basic process is that when you complain to the WRC, they first try to mediate a solution. Someone calls you, then they call the employer and they go backwards and forwards listening to both sides and making suggestions until everyone is happy – more or less. If they can't mediate a solution then you have the option of going to adjudication, where both sides sit down in a room together for a hearing with someone whose job is to make a ruling.

Adjudication is voluntary; you can go to court if you prefer but if you've refused adjudication then the judge is going to want to know why. The whole point of adjudication is that it's a lot less formal than a court hearing, you don't need a lawyer and it's free. The process is designed to be accessible to ordinary people so that employers don't have an advantage. The rulings have the force of a legal judgment.

CPL's offer was quite laughable. I sent Maria a message to say that the game was afoot. CPL seemed to be on the defensive, so she rejected their offer and we waited to see what would happen next. I don't recall CPL coming back with a revised offer and a few months later we had moved on from mediation and had an adjudication hearing scheduled. However, a day or two before that hearing they came back to us offering Maria a sum of money that she was happy with. There was a lot of last-minute wrangling with CPL's lawyers trying to add all kinds of clauses to the WRC's standard settlement agreement. In the end, we didn't close the deal until we were at the WRC building and late for the hearing.

CPL's people were in one room, we were in another, and the WRC staff were running backwards and forwards from one to the other like diplomats trying to end a war. It was tremendously fun, especially for Maria. After months of being treated as a criminal and having her arguments ignored, now she was calling the shots. She had brought CPL to the negotiating table, and now they were trying to appease her. It was fantastic.

Under the terms of the settlement, Maria is not allowed to talk about it. I guess the whole point was that CPL didn't want a ruling against them by the WRC because that would be public and damage their reputation. However, I didn't sign anything, and ultimately CPL didn't honour their side of the bargain to the letter. Signing the settlement was not the end of the matter as it should have been.

They were supposed to send Maria a payment within a month, but they never contacted her to confirm the logistics. About a week before payment was due she gave me her bank details and I forwarded them to CPL's lawyers – we didn't have any direct contact details for whoever was dealing with it at CPL – together with a reminder. They replied that everything was under control, but on the appointed day Maria called me in tears because she hadn't been paid.

We waited another day, so there could be no doubt CPL was in breach of the agreement, and then I called CPL's switchboard and asked to be put through to the office of Anne Heraty, the CEO and founder of the company. I spoke to her PA, who told me she knew absolutely nothing about this and promised to sort it out. Maria's money was transferred the same day and that was the end of it. At last.

Sadly, the other woman who was fired at the same time for the same offence wasn't able to get any justice. Like a great many CPL employees, she was from an immigrant background and didn't feel comfortable challenging authority in this way. Claims for unfair dismissal must be brought within six months, so by the time she heard about Maria's success, it was too late for her to get her courage up.

Since then I've been contacted many times by people who've been treated similarly by CPL. Very often the problem is simply that Facebook can't be bothered to make the effort to understand what's going on and just inform CPL that they don't want that person around any more. Then CPL has gone through the motions of an investigation, confident that the employee will just suck it up and leave without fighting their corner.

Only a very few of them have ever tried to bring a case to the WRC, even in clear-cut circumstances, with a very simple, accessible process and me encouraging them. My lawsuit, which requires me to prove wrongdoing by Facebook in the High Court, is a much more challenging and scarier proposition – not to mention potentially very expensive. I'm doing it because I'm older, more bloody-minded and not afraid to fail. I'm not concerned that a future employer might type my name into Google and discover that I'm a trouble-causer. Unfortunately, for a habitual employee, especially someone trying to build a life in a new country, I can see that getting justice is a very daunting prospect.

This whole episode illustrates how big companies can normalise deviation; someone bends the rules and gets away with it, and it happens again and again until it becomes 'just the way we do things around here'. Whether it's low-level staff improvising workarounds to gaps in the system or their managers ignoring rules and laws that were put in place for everyone's benefit, the rot spreads until nothing works properly.

Ultimately it's a failure of leadership. Everyone at every level is following the lead of the people above them. If your client requires that people get fired just for doing their jobs as they've been taught, and nobody is taking a principled stand, pretty soon it becomes routine to treat people badly and disregard your legal and ethical obligations to them.

Maria's case perfectly illustrates how Facebook's philosophy treats content moderators as disposable parts in a machine without recognising the skilled and nuanced work they do. They try to boil skilled judgement calls down to simple yes or no answers with no room for interpretation, from whether to investigate a suspicious user's activities to whether to fire someone for doing their job.

NINE

ANATOMY OF A SALE

As time went by, I was becoming increasingly frustrated on-site at Facebook because I could see problems and couldn't do anything about them. I don't have the 'keep your head down and work around the problem' gene. For most of my career, it has been my job to say, 'This needs to be changed to get a better outcome', and usually 'change' means getting someone to do something differently. This is what teachers do every day, and it's what we do as business or salespeople every time we meet a client.

I face the same problem today in trying to get justice from Facebook that I did when I was working on-site: how do I persuade people to change, how do I help them reach the decision I want them to? In other words: how do I sell that change to them?

I usually do it by following a process that has been refined and proven to work: taking them on a journey from where they are to where I want them to be. I'm going to walk you through that process – through a checklist of all the things that need to happen before Facebook announces a major reform of their thinking on the working conditions of content moderators, and why I think that is unlikely.

I'm presenting it as a linear process. It's easier to understand that way, but it's not really how it works, especially in complex situations. Everything I describe here is dependent on everything else, so it's more like a water-powered computing machine, driven by a collection of containers that all need to be kept filled up. Some of them leak, some of them connect to each other, and you have to run around adding water in different places until suddenly everything comes together and the wheels start turning.

It's perfectly possible to do everything listed here in five or ten minutes in the right circumstances. On the other hand, I have had sales calls that lasted three or four hours and you can think of your entire career as a long iterative sales process, so it's a useful tool.

To start with, you need to talk to the right person: the decision-maker. Take control of the conversation, establish your credibility and build some rapport with them. If they trust you enough to let you take the lead, then talk to them about why they're having this conversation with you. You want to understand their motivations and close in on the problem they want to solve. After they've acknowledged they have a problem, the conversation moves to defining it more clearly, and then to identifying why it's urgent. What pain is the problem causing them?

Next, you need to identify what factors have prevented

them from taking action so far. You're looking for the barriers that will prevent you from making a sale. Once you've isolated those, you can move on to asking them to define what the ideal solution would look like. You want them to draw up a checklist, and if you can tick all the boxes, you should have a sale. Present your solution and, once they see that it does everything they want, only then can you talk about price. If they have a problem that's causing them pain, and you have just offered them a solution, the discussion is about what it's worth to them to make the pain go away. Find the right price and you can close the sale.

After making the sale, you don't want them to get buyer's remorse and come back asking for a refund. You want to sell them something else in future. You don't want them bad-mouthing you to other people. You want them to introduce new customers. Closing the sale is not the end: it's the point where you start working on consolidating it and building on the relationship to move your agenda forward in future.

Most of the time I fell at the first fence with CPL. My little chat with Pedro in Chapter 6 was the only time I dealt with a decision-maker – the rest of the time I was effectively talking to the switchboard operator, whose job is to prevent sales calls from ever reaching the important people. The TLs and managers I dealt with were as powerless as I was; they didn't make the decisions and my naive efforts at problem-solving were a waste of time because of Facebook's status-based culture, its obsession with compliance and enforcement, and CPL's 'don't ever give the client bad news' mentality (all of which starts with Mark Zuckerberg keeping total control). This is the first hurdle I need to clear if I want Facebook to engage with the problem I've brought to their attention. In one sense, Facebook is an extension of one man's will. He is the decision-maker I need to talk to, but he doesn't want to talk, and it seems likely from his public comments that his understanding of the work of content moderators is quite limited. I can only blame the people around him for that.

Anyone who has ever tried to sell anything to large companies will know about 'screen queens': those people who answer the phones on behalf of the person you want to talk to and evaluate whether you're worthy of talking to their boss. Zuckerberg also has people screening his calls and emails, filtering the information that reaches him and deciding what's important for him to know about.

This brings me to my other understanding of Facebook. We talk about it as if it is a monolithic organisation (Zuckerberg does nothing to dispel that idea) but I've seen plenty of evidence in internal discussions that there are many factions and vested interests. There is competition between these parties for resources and prestige – it's how the organisation seems to function – so who exactly do I need to sell to? Who are the real decision-makers?

At the moment it seems like there is a long chain of them, all feeding information that fits their own agendas to the people above. I can't participate in that information flow because I have been characterised as a troublemaker, an ex-employee with a grudge, someone who is, in Zuckerberg's words, a little over-dramatic. I'm not credible, so I can't build a rapport with or gain any commitment from whoever makes the decisions.

This was also my problem with my CPL managers. I was talking about problems that were above the pay grades of the people I was talking to who were only concerned with winning compliance from me, not looking for change, and they couldn't acknowledge that I had any credibility anyway.

When TL Bill told me nobody cared what experience or skills I could offer in service of the quest to improve my team's quality scores, he wasn't simply quoting company policy or shutting down a troublemaker. I realise now that he was out of his depth. Just as I was treating people badly in Germany all those years ago, demanding compliance because I had nothing else to fall back on, he was similarly throwing his weight around to compensate for his inadequacies.

Throughout this book, I've used words like 'panic' several times to describe management decisions, and I don't think it's even a little over-dramatic to say that. These were people who had nothing in their management toolbox other than obtaining compliance and when that didn't work they just didn't know what to do.

Sometimes I try and imagine what would have happened if, like the dearly departed Pedro, the low-level managers I was dealing with had been more empowered and more skilled, not just focused on enforcing orders coming down from MPK in

Zuckerberg's name. If they had bought into the idea that if you're doing everything right as a manager your entire team can't fail repeatedly for months, what would have happened then? What would have been the barriers to taking action?

That's a hard one. For them to be empowered and better trained would imply a different relationship with Facebook, one in which they could send a message to their superiors explaining that there was some systemic problem. It would mean that I, my team and the management structure above me had all been hired to do expert work and now we were giving expert advice. Instead of 'this guy's behaviour is a problem' or 'these people's quality scores are a problem', the conversation would have become 'what is the problem that is causing these symptoms?' The way forward might have been a bit more palatable under those circumstances. However, I was just a nobody rocking the boat and struggling to overcome resistance from people who didn't want to listen.

All that's changed now is that the stakes are higher. My mission (in a nutshell) is to persuade Facebook to give all content moderators a 400 per cent pay rise, set aside a few billion to settle the claims of people who have been harmed to date and overhaul their system of content moderation.

It's a big ask, and the real price is one nobody acknowledges: what would it say about decisions made in the past by some very senior people, including Mark Zuckerberg himself? People would have to admit failure and I don't see any appetite for that within Facebook right now. The money is only a small part of the challenge I'm facing. The bigger issue is that the people who matter are not prepared to admit fault. I need to offer them some incentive, to solve a problem for them.

As far as I can tell, Facebook seems to think that they have already solved their content moderation problem. All of their PR statements on this matter are about incremental improvements, refinements to processes and small tweaks. I'm not offering them anything: I'm just making claims they reject. This brings us to another danger: liability.

Facebook has settled all kinds of claims from different people and governments by making payments on a no-fault basis and by signing agreements that ensure nobody is held accountable for anything. I suspect that my uncompromising public pronouncements have alarmed them, and the lawyers have jumped in to sell their solution.

Imagine you're a decision-maker at the highest levels of Facebook management, and you have somehow read the letter of claim sent by my lawyers in 2019 (or the one sent by Selena Scola a year earlier in California[†]) and you are concerned that, erm, your organisation may be doing something that could be done better. You raise this concern in a meeting and suggest that the best course of action is to engage with these claims and see what can be learned. You're not afraid to move fast and break things, and you believe in the possibility of radical change, what the tech industry calls disruption of the status quo.

† Selena's case is discussed in more detail in Chapter 11.

I imagine that in that situation, you would be treated as a heretic. The 'move fast with stable infrastructure' crowd would be outraged and the accountants would be screaming that if we admit to any failure or wrongdoing we could be on the hook for huge amounts of money. What would that do to the share price?

Everyone in the room has shares in the company worth, at least tens of millions of dollars. There's a moment of silence while they all consider this and their legal obligation to maximise profits for all the other shareholders. Then the legal person speaks up – the expert in the room on issues of liability and blame.

They're there to protect the company and its share price. They can't do that and can't commit to defending the status quo if they haven't already committed to the fundamental rightness of the company's values and activities. For them, it's an article of faith that nobody has been harmed and the company is not guilty of any wrongdoing.

What's more, they have a job to do – this is their raison d'être. They exist to refute everything I say, enforce NDAs and ensure that nothing embarrassing or harmful about the company is ever revealed, no matter what the truth may be. If they didn't forcefully defend the company against any and all comers, they wouldn't be doing their jobs, and you don't get a seat at the top table by being anything less than fully committed to your role.

The arguments against any kind of reasonable response are

made in terms of danger to the status quo, to the people at that table and to their constituencies. The arguments are made by people skilled at making their case, couched in legal terms that emphasise obligations to important stakeholders, without any consideration for the less powerful.

That's what I'm up against. It's an interesting conundrum and a professional challenge. It seems insurmountable, but I remain convinced that with some persistence and intelligence I can get the system to see sense. Maybe the drip of negative publicity will empower some factions within the empire. Maybe a copy of this book will fall into the hands of someone who matters and make enough sense that they reconsider their position. Or maybe I'll have to wait until a succession of judges in Ireland, and maybe at the EU level, have all ruled that Facebook has knowingly endangered content moderators by exposing them to harmful material without proper support.

Whatever it is that precipitates change, it will come. I'm going to win, and all that Facebook gets to decide is how much negative publicity – and associated regulations – they have to endure first. It would be cheaper and easier for them to just throw in the towel today and I hope the judges and their shareholders will consider that when reaching their verdicts.

TEN

SHOVELLING SHIT UPHILL

generally have a reputation for positivity at work. It's something that people comment on when they work with me. I don't see any point in staying at a job that you hate and reason that if I haven't left yet then I must like it. Hence, I always follow the maxim of 'be happy in your work'.

I've tried to be fairly upbeat about my first six months at CPL Onsite Facebook. Sure, there was plenty to complain about, just like in any job, but I have tried to communicate that I generally pushed on in the belief that all problems could be solved.

The enthusiasm and excitement of the early days, when we were all there to save the world in partnership with a prestigious and trusted brand, had waned. It slowly morphed into a commitment to do the best we could within the limitations of a system that was still evolving. At a certain point, it simply became a grim determination to keep going, to struggle on regardless. It was becoming increasingly clear that the system was stuck and we were stuck within it.

The idiocy of the NGO debacle stopped being a funny example of management incompetence to laugh about in the canteen and became a burden that we resented. Discussions about the meaning of a post became less vibrant and less frank; we were more concerned with defending our interpretations than with improving them. In short, the joy had gone out of it. When we started, we were protecting the innocent and fighting evil, infused with enthusiasm and confidence. Now we were just shovelling shit uphill and it was rolling back down onto us.

The fact that I was clinging on in a situation where I was desperately unhappy shows just how much I had lost sight of my core values at this time.

At least it was Christmas. My wife had invited her family to visit from Indonesia, so we had a flat full of freezing guests who had never visited a Western country before and we had to coordinate our days off to keep them entertained. She had moved on from Facebook by this time and had a bit more flexibility than me. Unfortunately, people don't stop posting nasty stuff during the festive season,[†] and CPL had to maintain the same level of service for the client, so time off was in short supply. We made it work for a week or so; I drove them up to Belfast to see the Titanic exhibition one day and she took them shopping in Dublin the next. At least one Guinness was

---

† This is when I met 'George' for the first time. He had been given that name by the day shift when videos of his murder were widely shared on Facebook and appeared in the queues regularly for a few weeks. I first watched his brutal stabbing a couple of days after Christmas. I remember a colleague saying, 'Oh, George is back,' like greeting an old friend, then 'That's not violating; don't delete it'. (Since there were no 'visible innards' and the victim was not fully incapacitated by the end of the video, he was not confirmed to be dead.)

supped while my hijab-wearing mother-in-law danced to trad music in Temple Bar, and someone raided my wardrobe while I was at work and started wearing all of my wool jumpers at once to keep warm.

I was still working with the day shift, but we were largely unsupervised over the festive season and the pressure was off for a while. It was a good time and it got better because I took all my accumulated holiday days at once and we flew to Spain together for a couple of weeks at the beginning of January.

I needed this trip, not to blow off steam but to recover my equilibrium. I'm at my best in challenging situations, helping people, adapting and using my initiative to solve problems as they arise. Herding tourists around a foreign country was exactly the kind of challenge that would remind me of who I was. For two weeks I was immersed in logistics, cultural challenges, sightseeing, shopping and the never-ending quest to find food that my Indonesian mother-in-law would eat. All difficult, all frustrating in their own ways, all solvable.

One day we were going to the Alhambra in Granada, a beautiful old town that was largely built before there were any cars. My wife doesn't drive so I was behind the wheel of a rented car, and Google Maps was telling me where to go. Follow this road, cross this one and then take a shortcut down this narrow lane …

I hesitated at the entrance because it looked very narrow and asked her majesty if she was sure this was the right road. She, not being a driver, looked at the map and told me to carry on, so I did and it soon became apparent that big tech had let me down again. The road was just about wide enough for two small vehicles and there were cars parked at intervals along one side so we had to squeeze past them. No problem. Not at first. Just ask everyone to breathe in and think thin so that we could get our big estate car through.

At one point we had to fold the wing mirrors in before we could pass. It was terribly tight and seemed to be getting tighter but there was nowhere we could turn around so we pressed on ... until we came to the steps. Yes, the steps. Google had sent me down a road that ended with a flight of steps. There was no way down and no way to turn around, and I couldn't even see out of the windows to reverse because of all the people and bags in the back of the car.

I still remember the strained silence as everyone sat there wondering what was going to happen next. I had snapped at my guests a couple of times in Dublin because of small things and to them this looked like a disaster. Worse, my wife had told me to drive down this road. Was this going to be her fault? It seemed like the perfect time and place for a massive row and blame-fest.

I got out of the car silently, but also very calmly, for a quick poke around to look for a solution. If I were in a little Fiat 500 like everyone else on the street I could have turned around, but we had a tank and it was longer than the road was wide. I could see that there was no option except to drive it backwards half a mile, and my calm magically turned to cheerfulness, optimism even. I grinned at my wife, hands in my pockets, and said something like, 'This is going to be fun. I need you to help me.'

Looking back, I think I was delighted to face a challenge like this. Undoubtedly it was difficult but the key difference was that I knew how to respond to it. After months of banging my head against a brick wall and depending on people and systems that weren't adequate, everything was suddenly very simple. It was a straightforward matter of skill and teamwork: get it wrong and you scrape the car along a wall or get it wedged irrevocably; get it right and you can walk away nonchalantly as if you do this kind of thing every day.

Everyone got out of the car and I drove it backwards through the obstacle course, preceded by my lovely wife. She warned me of obstacles, acted as a second pair of eyes as I eased the car through the gaps, offered praise and encouragement and generally impressed the hell out of her family with the way we dealt with the situation as they trailed along behind the car.

We missed the time slot we had reserved to see the inside of the Alhambra, but I still got about 2,000 photos of people posing around the exteriors and they were happy, so the day turned out well. Over next few days, we went skiing in the Sierra Nevada, we went to the bullring at Ronda, we ate about a hundred variants on the theme of paella and then we slowly meandered to Barcelona FC and La Sagrada Familia before saying goodbye.

It was a good experience, a reminder of who I was and an important break in the ever-worsening drudgery I had somehow volunteered for, but all good things must come to an end. In mid-January, I was back at my desk in the Beckett Building, this time with a little more clarity but not much more hope.

—

Almost as soon as I returned, we were called into a big meeting with several other teams to meet the new big boss. She subscribed to the 'management by intimidation' school and made it very clear before we even started that she was out for blood. Up to that point, the most senior person in the building had been 'Karen', the one who had just fired Maria. Now she had a boss and my first sight of this woman was her giving Karen a dressing down in public for being two minutes late to the meeting.

I didn't have a lot of affection or respect for Karen, but from a purely academic perspective, I have to say that it's not good to let your underlings see you humiliating your senior team. I don't know what she was compensating for, but she clearly felt the need to assert herself and make sure we all knew we were now answerable to someone who didn't care what anyone else might think.

That was the theme of the meeting. There was no attempt at getting to know anyone or presenting the best version of herself: our new boss launched straight into criticisms and laying down the law. She was very explicit: don't ever contact anyone from Facebook, even on the tribes that were there for us to ask them questions … don't ever give anyone any feedback other than bland platitudes. Not even the food. Don't make requests or let them know your preferences: just be grateful you get this perk. Under no circumstances should you ever embarrass your employer by doing anything that Facebook could interpret as complaining or causing trouble.

She did give us some good news. There was a pay rise in the works and the possibility of bonuses. It was a minimal rise, less than inflation, and accompanied by a new rule about quality scores. Whereas before we had previously been expected to achieve 98 per cent accuracy, the new number would be 99 per cent – so now we could only make half as many mistakes as before.

We headed back to our desks in silence. Things were not getting any better, and the morale of the team fell even more while I tried to hold on to the good mood I had brought back from my holiday.

What with Christmas and the trip to Spain, it was already a full month since the review where they had extended my probation. Maria had been fired while I was away, so that situation was no longer complicating things. I felt safely distanced from the events of the previous year and also less concerned about losing my job. A few weeks away had given me a sense of perspective. I was someone who solved problems and I remembered that if the problem is a difficult customer then my favourite solution is just to find a better customer.

I had money in the bank and access to social security for the first time in twenty years. I could afford to lose this job and that knowledge meant that nobody had leverage over me. If you don't have to worry about consequences you are free to reset your expectations and stick to your guns.

That was my theory anyway. In reality, as soon as I returned to the office it closed in on me again like a pervasive fog. I remembered what I had decided would be my attitude before coming back, but my emotions took over almost immediately. At the back of my mind was an acceptance that I had no long-term future in my job, but the front of my mind was consumed with the need to make my numbers. I had productivity targets to reach and a quality score to maintain or improve, and I was supposed to be on some kind of PIP – personal improvement plan – because I had been accused of behaving badly. The pressure was back on within a few hours of my return as if I had never been away.

I didn't pursue the PIP, why would I? It was just a bullshit excuse dreamt up by HR to warn me off from supporting Maria at the end of her investigative process. We also had a new team leader and I assumed he would have it on his to-do list anyway.[†]

[†] I don't know exactly what happened to TL Damien, but I suspect he was blamed for the systemic issues we had faced in the previous months. In any case, he disappeared from our lives and was never mentioned again. I did talk to him a long time later and he described the job as 'mental torture', with unreasonable expectations from the people above him. He also told me that he wasn't allowed to manage the team the way he wanted to, describing himself as a 'puppet'.

Of course, he didn't have it on his to-do list because nobody had told him about it. He didn't know that he was managing somebody whose probation had been extended or that there was any problem for him to deal with. The first he heard of it was when I brought it up in a meeting that I requested a month later, towards the end of February 2018. By then I was just trudging along, doing my work in a state of mild despair and still wrestling with an issue that had been bugging me since October.

Consider this: my entire team was perceived to be underperforming from the time we came together until we integrated with the daytime shift. Now we were back to our routine and had little contact with the daytime shift, and our quality scores were declining once again just as the required standard was going to be raised. The problem had not been solved and the first responder in this situation was supposed to be our team's coach.

You may recall that I had applied for this position when it came up and that it had gone to someone else. That person had been deemed ineffective by somebody when we started working with the day shift – it wasn't clear who as we didn't have an official TL at the time. Our coach wasn't allowed to coach but had not been replaced, so nobody – literally nobody – was taking responsibility for helping any of us to improve our declining quality scores. None of this made any sense at all.

One day I came into work and was greeted by a very sobering sight. We always arrived before the daytime shift had finished and would exchange a few pleasantries during the handover. However, this time I arrived to find a couple of my Eve10 colleagues standing nervously to one side and looking at a half-empty section. There was dead silence, none of the usual interaction or banter.

Half of the day shift team had been fired that afternoon because their quality scores were too low. One by one, they had been called into meeting rooms and then walked unceremoniously to the front door without even having a chance to say goodbye. These were the people to whom we were being compared unfavourably, also our friends, and now they were being slaughtered. Management, presumably our new big boss, had lost the plot completely and forgotten they weren't supposed to bring knives to work. They were slashing wildly, sacrificing anyone who even looked at them in a funny way. Those who remained were terrified.

—

Not long after this 'afternoon of the long knives' I sent my new TL a polite email asking if there was anything I could do, even unofficially, to help with the training situation. I reminded him that I had years of experience in adult education and might be able to offer some insights. It was this email which led to the meeting where I asked him about the PIP I was supposed to be on, and it went very badly.

Actually, there was one new initiative which had been introduced across the board a few weeks earlier. Every evening, at maybe 11 p.m., there would be a kind of surgery where a few select coaches and quality analysts would be available to answer questions on difficult moderating decisions for anyone who showed up. They had drawn up a rota, and from memory, I think there were two of them on duty for 30 minutes every night.

This might sound like a useful resource, but our problem was not that we regularly encountered things we didn't know how to process. Our problem was that we would make a decision that made sense, and then our auditors would sometimes make a different decision. The auditors would often disagree with each other, so it's not like we were making objectively incorrect decisions every time; the content we were dealing with was just very nuanced and subjective. We didn't know in advance which content was going to cause a problem, so there wasn't much point in taking it to these coaches.

However, our new TL insisted that every evening we send two members of our team to see them and that everyone should post examples of questionable content in our team's tribe for them to ask about. We complied and I remember taking my turn, sitting dutifully with my laptop open in front of us as I showed them the work that was our bread and butter. There was a moment of embarrassed silence as they looked at each other. Then one of them said, 'I've never seen anything like this.'

So it went, evening after evening. Two members of my team would go and sit with coaches from teams that didn't have to deal with the kind of hate speech and bullying we were immersed in. Then they would come back and post in the tribes that the coaches didn't have any advice or had agreed with the decision already made or had suggested that we implement some other rule altogether. This last suggestion was usually met with indignation and derision.

I'm making it sound like these people were incompetent, but they weren't. They were specialists in their markets being asked for opinions on behaviours and posting styles that they weren't familiar with, in a foreign language. The ESLA (Spain and Latin America) market, for example, spent most of their time dealing with sexual content and didn't encounter a lot of the nuanced hate speech that we did. We were the team that dealt with English-language content and so we were coming to them with questions that required an understanding of Scottish slang or Northern Irish politics. It was unfair to them, as well as a waste of everyone's time.

Pretty soon we were actively resisting. We started to look for content that we knew they would have difficulties with and that we would have to explain to them, just to make the point. Every evening we would each post, with a sly wink to the people sitting nearby, questions that we knew how to answer but that would collectively waste half an hour of coaching time. Ostensibly they were good questions, but we specifically looked for stuff that would elicit responses the auditors and quality specialists would contradict the next day, eventually putting an end to the whole stupid practice.

This solution wasn't helping, but when I had my PIP meeting and sat down with my new TL to discuss other ways to support myself and my team, he replied that nobody on my team was good enough to do the coaching job. Instead, he was going to bring in someone from another team, one of these people who had never had to deal with the content that was proving so problematic.

It's probably unfair to blame him for this. He had only been with us for a few weeks and had never done content moderation either, so I'm sure he was just repeating the company line and didn't know what he was talking about. Unfortunately, I had stopped caring about being reasonable.

Up to now, this book has been all about not being able to achieve anything and not being able to influence decisions. It was frustrating, but I was aware of the problem, understood it and still believed I could win. What I didn't understand at the time was that I was simultaneously struggling with the content I was seeing. I wasn't ready, emotionally, to understand that being exposed to the worst of humanity every day can affect you in profound ways and undermine your capacity to cope with the everyday stresses of life. Before I could accept this I had to go through all the drama of a public breakdown, months of spiralling despair and all the rest of the stuff I'll describe in later chapters. That was in the future. Right there and then I was in the grip of a mental breakdown I couldn't see.

Under normal circumstances, I'm quietly authoritative when trying to get someone to change their behaviour, but not reticent about expressing disappointment or disapproval quite eloquently if it seems necessary. You can't solve a problem if you let people pretend everything's hunky-dory. You have to get their attention and take control of the conversation. I will tell people truths they don't want to hear and be somewhat forceful about it if they don't want to listen.

However, I always keep myself under control, stay rational and focus on 'what is the problem and how are we going to solve it?' I'll walk out without a win, but with my self-respect intact, and sometimes I get a call back later – which is all part of the strategy.

Except in this meeting.

The reply about bringing in an outsider as our coach was just too much. All the frustration finally got the better of me and I didn't respond as I had intended, the way I normally would, the way that years of sales and teaching have taught me is most effective. Instead, I got horribly emotional, I couldn't reason clearly, I lost my temper, and I was all rage, bitterness and blame, complaining that 'Bill had fucked me.' I wasn't rational and I wasn't under control.

Of course, I wasn't able to change anyone's mind, the whole thing was a mess and I walked out of the Wubbalubbadubdub meeting room with murder in my heart.

—

Some months later I sent a subject access request (SAR) under GDPR to both Facebook and CPL, to obtain copies of any information they were storing about me. Among the documents I eventually received was a copy of an email describing this meeting. The name of the sender and the person it was addressed to had been redacted but the subject line was 'Chris Gray possible termination'. When I showed it to my therapist she replied that it described classic symptoms of PTSD – an overactive fight or flight reflex which overrides the reasoning part of the brain and leaves the individual unable to function rationally when they feel threatened.

I had exhibited symptoms of PTSD and my team leader wasn't trained or equipped to respond appropriately. I didn't know at the time that this email had been sent, and I was too far gone to have any insights into my mental state, but I was pretty sure I had just signed my own death warrant. I was on the way out and I knew it. This made me feel a lot better.

I described myself earlier as 'trudging along', which is a pretty good word to use for anyone stuck in a crappy job during an Irish winter. The days are short and sunlight is rare. It's cold and it rains a lot, so you walk around with your head down and your hands in your pockets, resisting the weather. This kind of body language has an awful effect on your mood and if you bring it into work with you it's like being in a constant state of resentment.

If it would just get properly cold it would be okay – real winter with snow and blue skies is a joy – but that rarely happens on the Emerald Isle. When it does happen, nobody knows what to do. The whole country shuts down, public transport stops, offices close and shops run out of food. It's like the end of the world, and as February 2018 turned into March, that was what we were facing. Storm Emma, the Beast from the East, was coming, and the media was full of dire predictions of blizzards. Everyone from the AA to the Met Office to trade unions was advising people to hunker down, panicked shoppers were raiding supermarkets, and Facebook eventually gave CPL permission for us to work from home.

The message came through in the middle of our shift, at maybe nine or ten o'clock at night. The snow was already falling heavily and people were starting to fret about how they would get home when our TL suddenly informed us we could leave. He chose two or three people to be on duty the next day and told them to take their laptops home with them. The rest of us were to leave them on-site as usual.

I remember stopping what I was doing when he said this and suggesting that maybe we should all take our computers, just in case. I wasn't going to argue if the client only wanted a skeleton staff the next day (we were getting paid anyway), but if we were out of the office for more than a day then surely there was a chance we might all be needed? After all, people don't stop using social media if they're trapped at home, do they? There would still be stuff to moderate, and work to do. Better to have the option of calling everyone up if needed, no?

No, of course not. So I locked my computer away and scurried home. It was only a ten-minute walk for me. I knew there would be a warm bed waiting for me so I didn't mind the cold, and I was looking forward to the next day. My wife and I hadn't experienced a real snowfall since we lived in Istanbul some years before and Storm Emma promised to be a rare treat.

We weren't disappointed, and the following morning found us building snowmen and igloos outside our apartment building. The snow was deep and the sky was a clear blue with brilliant sunshine. Some of our neighbours had young kids, snowballs were thrown and we were all out there having a great time when my phone rang. It was my TL calling me from home. Now that the city was at a standstill and we were all not going back to the office for a few days he needed us to … work from home.

I bit my lip, trying not to laugh. This shouldn't have been necessary, but of course, it was no problem for me to walk ten minutes up the road to the office and get my laptop, so there was no point in giving him a hard time. I just told him to let me know when he was going to be there. Other people had to make much longer journeys, so it was up to them to decide the schedule if they were willing to come in at all.

By rights, every one of us should have refused to leave the safety of our homes and go out into a city that was wholly unprepared for such weather. However, some did and one of my colleagues crashed his car on the way in.

So I worked from home for the next few days, sitting at my kitchen table and shielding the screen from my wife and our lodgers at the time. We used to rent out our spare bedroom to help with the rent, and I couldn't have them looking at confidential data. It had been hammered into us in training, and again when we were asked to work from home, that user privacy and client confidentiality were centrally important. On no account were we ever to let anyone know what our work entailed. Remember this later. It's important.

After the snow melted and we all returned to the office, I decided that I had nothing to lose and requested a meeting with the regional manager. I didn't go into it with any hope or expectation of any kind of changing anything; it was more of an exercise in confirmation on my part, so I was not upset by the outcome. It was very brief, my message being this: in my teaching career, if an entire class was not performing as required, then I would have to consider two possibilities. The first was that my expectations were unreasonable, and the second was that there was something wrong with the way I was training them.

By analogy, if my entire team is not reaching the required quality score then we have to ask whether the requirement is unrealistic, whether the company has hired the wrong people en masse, or whether there is something wrong with the management and training of those people.

The response to that, predictably, was that the company had made available the appropriate training resources, and anybody who couldn't reach the required standard with the available resources was not suited to the job. So that was that. I walked away satisfied that there was no point in making any further effort to reason with these people and waited to see what would happen next.

—

Not long after, I got an email inviting me to my nine-month review. It was set for a Friday at 6 p.m., the start of my shift. I was pretty sure this was going to be the moment I got fired, so I devoted a bit of time to thinking about what would come next.

As I had said to Maria six months earlier, when facing a difficult situation, you have to imagine what the worst outcome is likely to be and then lean into it. Once you've got your head around that future you can prepare for it. It holds no fear and then you have a clear head while dealing with it, even a fighting chance of getting a better one.

I wanted to have the final word. I wanted to win in some way and to be heard. I spent the next two days poking around on internal message boards and in my chat history, taking screenshots of conversations which illustrated some of the problems I had faced on the job. I didn't have a coherent plan for what I was going to do with them, and I wasn't even thinking in terms of mental health, but I knew I was going to do something.

On the appointed day I pitched up at the security desk by the front door and apologised because I had forgotten my ID badge, which I needed to open internal doors or use the lifts. They gave me a temporary one, and I went up to my desk and faffed around for a few minutes putting my personal effects into the bag I had brought for that purpose. I then presented myself in the designated conference room to see what they had come up with.

It was a very short meeting, with my TL and the RM both appearing quite embarrassed and uncomfortable. You would think that people in an industry with such a high turnover and such a brutal hiring and firing policy would be used to this kind of thing but I realised later they had been afraid I would blow up and start shouting and screaming.

I didn't. I sat there politely and impassively listening while they explained that due to my quality score they, unfortunately, had to let me go. I may have even smiled slightly. I didn't point out that I had surveyed the rest of my team only the day before and was confident that my quality score was much the same as everyone else's. I didn't argue that the only reason they were having this meeting with me, and not with anyone else on my team, was that my probation had been extended three months earlier.

I simply asked for a statement of accrued holiday time that I would be paid for, on top of the two weeks' notice they owed me but weren't requiring me to work. TLs are supposed to keep records of this stuff because they're responsible for approving time off, but it seems mine hadn't done it. Instead, they replied that I should ask HR by email and, after a moment's contemplation, I let it pass. What was the point in arguing?

I left. That was it. There was no big dramatic exit, no 'take it or leave it' ultimatum, no sudden revelation that I needed to escape, no heroic confrontation. I was simply eased out by people who had concluded I was too difficult to manage. I was too weary to even protest.

I just disappeared from my desk, and my colleagues never saw me again. My TL escorted me downstairs to the front door in uncomfortable silence, and we shook hands with no hard feelings. Poor guy! Then he asked for my ID badge, so I handed him the temporary one security had given me 30 minutes before and went on my way, back to my very relieved wife.

Her immediate response when I turned up back at home less than an hour after leaving was a big grin. 'Thank God,' she said. 'You have become such a horrible person since you started that job. I want my husband back, the lovely guy I married!'

We went to bed early, both believing that would be the end of my Facebook story.

ELEVEN

SELENA

I would love to report that I slept the sleep of the just the night after I left the Beckett Building for the last time. Unfortunately, if your body is used to being at work until 2 a.m. then it's going to take a while to adjust back to normal. I was a bit discombobulated for the next week or so, but I faffed around contentedly and amused myself by writing to CPL to get a statement of holiday pay owed to me.

I also met up with Maria in the inevitable coffee shop. We had already prepared most of the paperwork for her to bring a case against CPL claiming unfair dismissal, and now that I was safe from repercussions we were both keen to get that under way. It took only a few hours to double-check everything and submit it online, and then it was a case of waiting to hear back from them so I could safely put it out of my mind.

I waited to hear back from CPL too. They owed me two weeks' paid notice, plus accrued holiday pay, and it was two weeks before my final payday. I wanted to be sure they had got it sorted so that I didn't have to have any interaction with them ever again. Of course, they muffed it up.

It was the usual story: nobody was responsible for anything, nothing was done properly and everyone just muddled through so when I got my final payslip a fortnight later it didn't make any sense at all. I was furious, and with nothing better to do with my time I sent an angry email straight to the person at the top – the new site manager who had been so combative in her 'welcome to me' meeting a few months before. I also copied in several other people in the upper echelons.

I didn't mince any words. I wanted to be paid, I was entitled to be paid, and all they had to do was pay me according to the contract. I wasn't asking for anything unreasonable, and this was an organisation with huge staff turnover. If you have 1,500 people in the building, and most of them last less than a year, then you should expect to be letting people go every day. You should have a system in place to do this quickly and efficiently, to ensure that everyone gets paid what they're owed without having to take up anyone else's time.

From what I had already observed, and heard from other people including my wife, it seemed like there was a deliberate policy of making it hard for departing employees to get a clear statement of what was due to them. Everyone I knew had been paid incorrectly at some point during their time with CPL as well, and these salary errors were always in CPL's favour. Nobody ever got overpaid: they were always short-changed. I wasn't going to tolerate any shenanigans on my way out the door.

I gave them a clear and short deadline with a warning that if I wasn't paid exactly correctly then I would be making my own complaint to the Workplace Relations Commission. They responded by ignoring this threat as well.

Much later on, as part of the SAR process under GDPR,

I saw copies of internal emails stating that I was correct, but there was no record of anyone taking any action.

If someone had just phoned me I would have waited longer, but they didn't and I had already learned how the WRC process worked. I wanted to get on with my life and couldn't do that without walking away from a big pile of cash. To make matters worse, when I registered with social services as unemployed, CPL gave them the date of my final payslip rather than the last date I worked, which deprived me of two weeks' social security.

So the deadline passed, and I immediately made good on my promise to involve the WRC. I sent the forms in, cc'd them to CPL … and within a few days I got paid everything that was owed. After months of playing the game and being treated badly, I had stood up to them and won. (Maria's case would take another six months to resolve and continued lurking in the background but it was not as urgent.) I was free to get on with my life at last.

I didn't rush to find a new job, though. I was oddly unmotivated and lethargic and having trouble adjusting back to a normal sleep pattern. I put this down to having worked strange hours for so long, but in truth, I wasn't having any problems going to bed at a reasonable time. In theory, I should have been sleeping eight or ten hours a night, but instead I was in bed for ten or twelve hours a day and never feeling rested.

My wife had always worked days, so for the entire period I was at CPL we were both dealing with disrupted sleep. She would go to bed at a normal time; I would come in at 2 a.m. and try not to wake her, usually unsuccessfully, because we weren't spending any quality time together, so this was our chance for a chat and a cuddle, or something. Our love life was, well, non-existent. I remember one night morosely scratching her back with the stubble on my chin, something that had once been an intimate and erotic act. Now it was me uncomfortably serving someone who was half-asleep with her back to me, scratching an itch without any passion on either side. Then I would be woken by her alarm in the early morning as she went to work and would have to try to get back to sleep with the sun shining in through the curtains.

I was always somewhat tired and dispirited and it had become normal. In the weeks and then the months after leaving CPL I didn't really think about it, but nothing changed. I was not sleeping well even though I was going to bed at ten o'clock. Instead of enjoying the spring sunshine, I remained tired and irritable, and this persisted even after I got a new job.

My period at CPL had shown me that I wasn't cut out to spend my days sitting in front of a computer, or even standing in front of one with a blanket around my shoulders and music blasting into my headset. I was used to being more active, having more freedom and responsibility, and also dealing with real people. I wasn't interested in teaching English again but I needed to find something in a similar vein. A few months later I was relieved to find the perfect fit; I would take groups of tourists around Ireland and teach them about the culture and history of my newly adopted country.

Every morning, I would load up to 50 smiling strangers onto a bus, lay down the law about not being late back when we stopped and regale them with just the right amount of information and jokes to ensure that when they returned to Dublin 14 hours later they would be completely satisfied.

They wanted to be listened to, respected, advised, guided, told and helped. Sometimes they also needed to be instructed, to know that someone was in charge and everything was under control. It was sales and teaching all over again, rapport and credibility, understanding what people want, being the smartest and most interesting person in the room one moment, being genuinely interested in them the next. It was a long day, but I made more money working four days a week than I did on five evening shifts for CPL. It was also a lot of fun.

Then, in September 2018, I saw a news story with the headline 'Facebook moderator sues over "beheading stress"' and stopped, fascinated.

The story was about a woman named Selena Scola, who had worked as a content moderator in California at almost the same time as I had been doing the same work in Ireland. Like me, she had worked for an outsourcing company and was not directly employed by Facebook. She was claiming to have been 'bombarded' with thousands of images depicting child sexual abuse, torture, bestiality and beheadings, which she alleged had left her with post-traumatic stress disorder.

I didn't know what to think. Fighting your ex-employer for unpaid wages, or because you've been unfairly fired, is one thing. This was next level and looked to me to be a cynical cash grab. I was aware that the US had a nonsensical legal system that meant people and corporations lived in constant fear of being sued to smithereens over inconsequential things, but PTSD? It seemed like a step too far.

I wouldn't have dismissed the idea of what used to be called shell shock or battle fatigue. I could understand that people who had faced life-threatening challenges and real, terrifying trauma might, in some circumstances, have flashbacks or nightmares but that was about my limit. If you had talked to me about ex-soldiers self-medicating or drowning their sorrows, well, I was an unruly boozer from my teens to my mid-forties. Who needed an excuse to get drunk? Why not just man up and admit that you go over the top sometimes? Or often? As for exposure to extreme content, well, that was just ridiculous. It hadn't affected me. I was fine.

As far as I was concerned, this was just some chancer who had found a lawyer willing to try to squeeze some money out of a big company in the name of an imaginary illness. It was interesting and audacious and I admired her chutzpah in trying it. I wondered how much she was hoping to get, and I must confess I did wonder if there was any way I could get in on the action. It wasn't a serious thought, though. How would I convince an expert there was something wrong with me in the first place? I wouldn't know where to start, and I'm a lousy actor so I forgot about it.

I wanted to put my time with CPL behind me, and life on the buses was pretty good. It was a 14-hour day in the sense that I had to be there to glad-hand the guests before loading them at 7 a.m. and didn't get back to Dublin until eight or nine at night, but I wasn't 'on stage' for much of the time. I would get everyone settled, do the safety talk and tell them a bedtime story to make them sleep while we drove – usually a potted history of the last ten thousand years in Ireland.

Then I would read, listen to podcasts or chat with anyone interesting I found on the bus until we got close to our first stop and I had to pick up the mic again. A quick briefing, some local history, dire warnings about being back on the bus in time and then I could go take a walk in nature, enjoy a leisurely breakfast or sleep for an hour or two while they did their exploring. Then on to the next stop and repeat.

I took some kind of siesta almost every day because I still wasn't sleeping well at night. I should have been able to get seven hours of sleep at night pretty easily but would often wake up after a few hours feeling washed out and tense. I never remembered my dreams or had a sense of having had nightmares but would lie there for hours in the dark thinking about nothing. I was on edge and tense, but I didn't know why and had no context for what was happening.

I was generally pretty good with the guests. I had all the basics under control and did the job mostly on autopilot.

I would put my professional face on, do a meet-and-greet, let them know I was in charge and generally be friendly and knowledgeable so they mostly just went along with whatever I told them. These were people who had outsourced their travel adventure and ceded control of the day to me, so as long as I met their expectations they rarely made any trouble. All I had to do was always have a plan, communicate clearly and give them just as much culture and history as they could handle.

Every few weeks I would get someone on the bus who didn't want to be there or thought they were the boss. Maybe they had been dragged along by family, had a hangover, had something else going on in their lives that was making them unhappy or were just plain spoilt. Whatever the reason, these people were trouble, and I struggled to deal with them. Whenever they pushed back, something strange happened. I would get a tingling in my scalp and speak more loudly and forcefully, and my body language would get more aggressive. As a result, things would never get resolved as smoothly as they should. Looking back, I can see that this was a classic threat response, my fight-or-flight reflex was being activated and my capacity to reason was diminished.

I had the same problem occasionally with drivers. We had to work closely together to juggle the expectations of the guests with the realities of traffic, weather and legal restrictions on how long the driver could spend behind the wheel at one time. If we were delayed on the road, that might mean cutting short the time we spent at one location or it could mean that we couldn't move until the driver had had his obligatory time off. We were in constant communication about how the day was going and how it was likely to go, what change I might need the guests to accept or how far I needed the driver to push the limits.

There was a lot of give and take required and occasionally these negotiations turned into heated arguments. I remember one guy looming over me with fists balled, red in the face; and I was staring him down, ready to go at it. This is totally unlike me. Thankfully it didn't happen very often but it did happen.

It happened enough that after a few months I left my job following an avoidable conflict. I joined another company and a few months later the situation repeated itself, so I found another one and it happened again. Three times in one year. At the time I blamed everyone else, but now I can see that I was a bit of a mess. I didn't have anything to fall back on when things went wrong.

Another thing that changed during the first year after leaving Facebook was that I stopped using their site, or any social media at all. I thought that I had just lost interest, that I had better things to do with my time, but it's more accurate to say that I was avoiding it. I remember, for example, a driver showing me a video clip someone had sent him on WhatsApp and looking away after a few seconds. I didn't want to look, whatever it was. I think I was anticipating something awful appearing and trying to avoid it.

Fortunately, I wasn't the only one who saw the news stories about Selena. My old pal 'Weird Alex' was another. He was let go by CPL in late 2018, and it didn't take him long to start looking for a lawyer in the hope of bringing a similar case in Ireland. He also tried to get journalists interested, and that eventually led to him phoning me and giving my number to Jennifer O'Connell of the *Irish Times*.

That was six months after Selena's story broke, but it would be fair to say that she started the ball rolling and I think it's important to talk about her case in some detail.

In September 2018 it was just Selena suing Facebook and she did it through the courts in San Mateo, California. The lawyers managing the case argued that it had the potential to become a class action. This means that the outcome could affect everyone who had ever been a content moderator in California without them having to bring a case.

The court filings describe her experiences in much the same language as my own writ would a year later. There was the same bad management, productivity and quality metrics, relentless awfulness and complete disregard for the possibility of anyone being harmed. Similar symptoms: the same sense of someone trying to come to terms with challenges they didn't understand. We had lived parallel lives.

Within a few months, there were more names on the claim. While Selena had worked in California, there were now plaintiffs who had worked in Arizona, Texas and Florida. These were the only four US states where Facebook had content moderation centres, all managed by the same few outsourcing companies, so these handful of former moderators were now representative of the whole industry (at least in the US).

The judge granted the case class action status, so the outcome would now apply to all content moderators in the US. Thousands of people were affected now, not just Selena and those few brave (or greedy) souls that had come forward. This was massive, and I wish I had been paying more attention at the time.

Think about this: a single individual takes on a giant corporation with enormous resources. How is that likely to turn out? To have any hope of winning they would need a huge team of their own, which is ridiculously expensive. How are they going to pay for it? What law firm is going to take that case unless they're being paid up front?

However, if your case attracts a lot of media attention, more plaintiffs come forward and you win class action status, the potential payout may be hundreds or thousands of times larger in total. The upfront investment to fight the case, in time, resources and salaries for legal staff remains much the same but now the total amount of money on the table is much, much larger. For a lawyer, a percentage of the payout as their fee suddenly looks very attractive.

At the same time, the big corporation has every incentive to crush an individual plaintiff. They know that they have all the money and power, so they don't need to play nice, and they don't. On the other hand, when a corporation is faced with a class-action lawsuit and an army of motivated lawyers who are all confident they have a chance of winning, that certainty goes away. Now there is an incentive to take this seriously and look for the cheapest way out.

If the company fights ten cases and calculates the odds of losing any one of them to be 50/50 and they will be fined a million dollars a time if they lose, that's an average $500,000 loss per case. Five million dollars in total, plus their legal fees. Could be more, could be less, but that's the most probable outcome. What if instead they just offered everyone $100,000 to go away? That would cost only one million dollars and lower legal fees.

The plaintiffs have to make the same calculation. They can hope to make a million dollars, minus their legal fees, after being dragged through the courts for years. On average, each plaintiff will get only half that amount. Or everyone can take $100,000 today and get on with their lives.

In class-action lawsuits all the incentives align so that both sides want to reach a settlement quickly, instead of dragging things out for years. There doesn't have to be any actual collusion between the two sides, but the respective legal teams all know how things work. It's like a dance. Everyone plays their part, everyone goes through the motions, boxes get ticked and an outcome is reached that everyone was hoping for.

Well, almost everyone. Everyone who matters, you could say. Just not the plaintiffs.

—

In May 2020, eighteen months after Selena started proceedings and a year after I had first contacted my solicitor, Dave Coleman, about my suit, it was announced that Facebook had settled the US class-action lawsuit. The payout was $52 million. For all of five minutes this sounded like great news: it set a precedent and gave us hope that we would be next in line for enrichment.

But when you consider that this offer was for all potential claims by anyone in the class, all current and former content moderators in the US, it stops sounding so great. There were over 11,000 potential claimants, so the settlement was worth an average of $5,000 each, and that's without taking the legal fees into account.

In the preliminary settlement lodged with the court on 11 May 2020, Selena's lawyers asked for $17 million as their fee, 32.7 per cent of the total payout. That comes off the top before anything is disbursed to the plaintiffs. This means the amount on the table is $35 million and that money is then lodged with a specialist claims administration company. This is a for-profit company that charges fees for managing the next step, leaving an average of around $3,000 for each person in the class.

I had to pinch myself as I read this, and then remind myself that not everyone who does content moderation gets PTSD. I read somewhere in the court documents and press releases that maybe 50 per cent of moderators were expected to make a claim, and I've seen other literature estimating that 20 or 30 per cent of people exposed to extreme content are affected. So, best guess, the average payout might be as high as $15,000.

By the time Dave Coleman called me, just a few minutes after the announcement hit the press, I was already in disbelief. We were laughing, of course – Facebook had paid out – but it was 'what the fuck' kind of laughter. It looked like an incredibly bad deal – a disaster for my American counterparts. I didn't have to tell Dave that I wouldn't be signing anything on those kinds of terms. But was that strictly true?

By speaking publicly, and being the lead plaintiff, I had become, to a certain extent, the face of content moderation in Europe. I spoke, more or less, for thousands of people who didn't dare to speak for themselves. I was fighting the good fight for them as much as for myself. What would I do if someone offered me $17 million to turn my back on them and accept a deal that left them hanging?

I wish I could say otherwise, but I would probably take the money and run. I've spent too long sitting in front of my computer writing this book and I need the exercise. It's all about incentives, and I can't see how Selena's lawyers could be incentivised to fight on for many years to get her a better deal. This looked like as good as it was going to get.

Selena will probably never work again in the tech industry, which is hard for someone living in that part of California. Imagine you apply for a job and pass the interview and then they type your name into Google. They will see that you once sued your employer, that you're a troublemaker, the kind of person who wants to fix things. How is that going to end? Not well, I suspect.

I assumed that this would be taken into account in the settlement and that Selena's earning potential would be reduced. Surely she too would have taken a slice out of the settlement before the other 11,000 moderators got a look-in?

No. She got $20,000 for giving years of her life, trashing her reputation and making herself almost unemployable in tech. That's not a misprint: I've double and triple-checked this. That was her reward as the lead plaintiff who set the ball rolling for everyone. Other plaintiffs, the ones from the other states who joined later, got $5,000 each. Their names are also given in the court documents, so anyone can find out what part they played.

To be clear, that is not all they got. Those payments were on top of whatever they are deemed to be entitled to by the claims management company as compensation. The way that works, incidentally, is as follows:

First, the claims manager sends an email and physical mail to everyone who has worked in the US as a CM for Facebook since 2015, notifying them of the class action and their entitlement and directing them to a special website. Every one of those people is entitled to request a one-time payment of $1,000, no questions asked. They can use this to seek a medical diagnosis if they think they might have PTSD or similar, but they're not required to. I imagine that pretty much everyone claims their $1,000 – I know I would.

Lastly, those who do obtain a diagnosis can then put in a claim for an additional payment. If there is enough money in the pot, the maximum payout is theoretically $50,000 per person in total, with a sliding scale of symptoms to determine what you're entitled to. If too many people claim, the individual payouts have to be adjusted downwards.

It all sounds just ... stingy. And it got worse. Here's some text from the settlement agreement:

WHEREAS, at all times, Defendant [Facebook] has denied and continues to deny (a) that it has liability for the claims and allegations of wrongdoing made in the Action by Plaintiffs or members of the Settlement Class, as defined herein; (b) all charges of fault, liability, and wrongdoing against it arising out of any of the conduct, actions, or omissions alleged or that could have been alleged in the Action; (c) that Plaintiffs or members of the Settlement Class have asserted any valid claims against Defendant; (d) that Plaintiffs or members of the Settlement Class were harmed by any conduct of Defendant alleged in the Action or otherwise; and (e) that the Action was, or properly could be, certified as a class action for any purpose other than settlement purposes in accordance with this Agreement;

WHEREAS, Defendant, without any admission or concession whatsoever and despite believing (a) that the Action cannot properly be certified as a class action for any purpose other than settlement purposes in accordance with this Agreement; (b) that it is not liable for the claims asserted against it in the Action; and (c) that it has good and meritorious defenses thereto, has nevertheless agreed to enter into this Agreement to avoid further expense, inconvenience, and the distraction of burdensome and protracted litigation and thereby to put to rest this controversy and avoid the risks inherent in complex litigation; and

WHEREAS Class Counsel have considered the arm's-length settlement negotiations conducted by the Parties and, based on their investigation of the facts, review of applicable law, and analysis of the benefits that this Agreement affords to Plaintiffs and Class Members, have concluded that (a) the terms and conditions of this Agreement are fair, reasonable, and adequate to Plaintiffs and Class Members; and (b) it is in the best interests of Plaintiffs and Class Members to settle the claims raised in the Action pursuant to the terms and provisions of this Agreement in order to avoid the uncertainties of litigation and to ensure that the benefits reflected herein are obtained for Plaintiffs and Class Members;

NOW, THEREFORE, IT IS HEREBY STIPULATED AND AGREED by and among Plaintiffs and Defendant, through their undersigned counsel, that, subject to final approval of the Court and in consideration of the benefits flowing to the Parties from this Agreement set forth herein, the Released Claims shall be finally and fully compromised, settled, and released and that

the Action as against Defendant shall be dismissed with prejudice, upon and subject to the terms and conditions set forth below.

Let me summarise that for you: Facebook denies any wrongdoing or liability, or that anyone has been harmed, but doesn't want the distraction and expense of continuing to fight the case. Here's some money to go away on the condition that this is the end of the matter. No moderator anywhere in the US can bring any further action against Facebook once this settlement is approved by the court.[†]

I struggled to see why Selena would have accepted it, but she wouldn't talk to me. When I tracked her down I got a very short reply stating that all communications should be through her legal team, at least until everything was settled.

I sat twiddling my thumbs and waited to hear that she had got her money and that it was all over. I wanted to hear about what had gone on, and why she had settled. So I waited.

And waited.

The settlement was announced in May 2020. A year later, in May 2021, it still hadn't received final approval. In fairness, Covid had caused some disruption, but this was ridiculous. Getting information was also a nightmare. The San Mateo Court website kept denying me access to the records on file because it had some insane geo-blocking system that identified me as a cyber-security threat. Their tech guys managed to give me access a couple of times, but whenever I went back to the site I hit the same firewall.

---

† Consider that Facebook made a profit of $39,370,000,000 in 2021. This is 757 times the cost of fobbing off 11,000 people who have been harmed by the work they did.

In December 2021, more than a year and a half after the settlement was announced, Selena finally got back in touch to let me know that she had been paid – a massive $21,000! She had her first no-questions-asked thousand plus her award as the lead plaintiff and now she was starting the process of trying to get whatever else she might be entitled to in compensation. The long wait was (almost) over. Finally, we could chat and compare notes.

Since then, we have had a lot of long and interesting conversations. I don't want to put words in her mouth, reveal anything confidential or leave her open to criticism or abuse. She's been through a lot and, in my opinion, has been treated pretty shabbily but I think it's safe to say that my initial assumptions about her were wrong.

I genuinely believe that Selena Scola was and is suffering from some form of stress disorder and that her work for Facebook is the cause of it. I am also convinced that her primary motivation for launching her lawsuit was to try to right a wrong and win better working conditions for other content moderators.

Of course she wanted to get paid – we all do (and we need to) – but first and foremost in our conversations is always the same theme that recurs throughout this book: a huge, arrogant company that doesn't know how to solve its content moderation problem, sacrificing people with about as much compassion as a kitchen hand dumping potatoes into the chipper.

Life as a CM is gruelling and debilitating and we're not allowed to talk to anyone about it. Life as one of the few CMs who have taken a stand is lonely and challenging. Selena is probably the only person I can talk to who understands what it's like to take up the torch and put yourself in the firing line, for years, to try to bring about change in a dysfunctional industry.

I'm tremendously grateful that we're able to talk at last, even if it's mostly to commiserate.

TWELVE

OUTSOURCED WELLNESS

F ollowing the announcement of Selena Scola's lawsuit against Facebook, the company issued a statement which was reported by the BBC on 25 September 2018. It reads:

> We recognise that this work can often be difficult. That is why we take the support of our content moderators incredibly seriously, starting with their training, the benefits they receive, and ensuring that every person reviewing Facebook content is offered psychological support and wellness resources. Facebook employees receive these in house and we also require companies that we partner with for content review to provide resources and psychological support, including onsite counselling – available at the location where the plaintiff worked – and other wellness resources like relaxation areas at many of our larger facilities.

This sounds great in principle, but what does it mean in

practice? Maybe it's time to dig into what 'wellness' actually means.

—

Some months after I left the job, as part of the process of helping Maria fight her case for unfair dismissal, we made subject access requests (SARs) to CPL and Facebook to get all the information they had about us.

I'll talk more about that process later, but the important thing now is that, although we got a lot of papers back in return, I was curious to note there were no records of my having any interaction with the wellness team. I didn't think too much of this omission at the time and assumed it was maybe something to do with patient confidentiality, but then I started to wonder. As I began to talk to journalists a year later, all of them asked about what kind of mental health support was provided by CPL. How do you support people whose daily work involved watching child abuse, graphic violence, torture, revenge porn, terrorist propaganda, ethnic cleansing, war crimes and much, much more? It was very much the topic of the day and eventually I had a look on LinkedIn for the counsellor I had talked with.

I was amazed to discover that her profile made no mention of CPL. It seemed she worked for a company called Zevo Health instead and was now a director of it. I suppose, in principle, this makes some sense. CPL provides low-skill low-paid labour to big tech companies. I can understand they may want to outsource specialist services like mental healthcare to experts, or even to sports psychologists.

Mind you, CPL is a huge company with many different divisions, some of which specialise in providing medical staff. Why would they not keep this in-house and use their own experts instead of allowing some other company to make a profit from them?

I went back to LinkedIn to confirm the name of the company the counsellor had worked for, but her profile had been taken down. A similar thing occurred the following year when CPL (now rebranded as Covalen) announced that they were hiring a clinical psychologist at last. I looked this psychologist up on LinkedIn as well and, amazingly, her profile vanished a few days later.

—

So CPL is outsourcing mental health support. What of it? I felt that it was worth looking into and I started with the Zevo Health website, which was squarely focused on marketing. There was a profound emphasis on staff retention and absenteeism (stuff that can be summarised as 'keeping people at their desks') and nothing at all about managing potential harm. A search of their site on PTSD turned up nothing.

I now knew why my SAR to CPL and Facebook had not turned up anything about wellness and counselling: I had asked the wrong company, so, obviously, the right thing to do was send an SAR to Zevo as well.

It took their CEO two weeks to reply, and his response was a short paragraph telling me to talk to CPL. They were my employers and they were the data controllers, not him.

I replied immediately with a strongly worded email stressing that I had already made an SAR to CPL and that now it was his turn and I threatened to involve the Data Protection Commission (DPC). Then I sent another one to the data controller at CPL. I had already been in contact with him about the data they were holding, and I made it very clear to him that I wanted Zevo's records from Zevo.

I eventually got records which proved that a) I had asked for help from the wellness team while working at CPL, b) it had taken weeks for them to set up a counselling session and c) they didn't make any notes about the session or take any action afterwards. It was a tussle, but I won that one small victory.

Since then, the T&S industry, in general, seems to have started coming to terms with the realities of the mental health challenges faced by content moderators. Even though legal departments continue to insist that nobody has or can be harmed, there is a lot more acknowledgement from professionals of the 'challenges' and 'risks', although it's rare for anyone to explicitly use words like 'trauma' or acknowledge PTSD. Zevo Health is, in fairness, something of a trailblazer in this regard, releasing a YouTube video in late 2021 titled 'What does wellbeing & resilience look like for content moderators?'

Here's a snippet from the transcript of that video, in which a counsellor is responding to another speaker:

Really valid point there, and it echoes a lot of what, you know, I myself have heard when speaking with content moderators: the sense of 'I'm fine, it doesn't affect me,' but there is that accumulation and that does occur over time. And we'll be talking to Dr Marielle Barcelo later on, so she'll be able to share some more of the effects that content moderation, or exposure to content, can have on an individual, and I think ... you know that point around, it's a ... it's a process of evolution, you know, the culture needs to change: it's not just that acceptance that this is the work and we have to get used to it. It's really about understanding how the work ... has potential for harm. And that's a great lead-in now to Jackie as well, and just in the work that you're doing around the prevention of psychological harm in content moderation.

The conversation goes on for over an hour and several different speakers talk openly and in detail about exactly the issues reported by people like me and Selena – issues which Facebook's legal department is still denying.

So, clearly there has been a shift in attitudes, although not as great as I would hope. Around the same time as they published that video, Zevo were also recruiting more counsellors, and I happened to see one of their ads. The headline was still 'Health Coach' but the detailed description indicated they wanted a 'fully qualified mental health practitioner' with all the appropriate accreditations. The job was not only to deliver mental health and well-being programmes but also to design them. They seemed to be taking the role seriously, and the first paragraphs even mentioned 'the latest empirical research'.

In addition to 'evidence-based psychological well-being training', it included the line 'adhere to the coach Code of Conduct to escalate risk situations'. This was all music to my ears. They were looking for a properly qualified person as well.

The minimum qualification was a master's in psychology with demonstrated mental health treatment and intervention skills, i.e., someone who could recognise trauma and intervene to provide help. Plus, training was needed in cognitive behavioural therapy. The applicant should have at least two years' experience working with adults since qualifying, including with people affected by or at risk of suicide. They should be able to work with groups and provide solution-focused interventions.

And these were just the minimum qualifications. On the 'desirable' list was a PhD in counselling psychology, motivational interviewing skills and Trust and Safety awareness. It looked as though there had been a sea change in how they thought about the impacts of doing content moderation.

The role was definitely related to my old job. It was even the same hours, 6 p.m. to 2 a.m., 'on the client's premises'. For one brief moment, it seemed that at last someone had come to their senses and accepted that people were being harmed by doing content moderation. Here was a genuine attempt to get a handle on that and find solutions.

And then I saw the salary: €30,000

Who in their right mind is going to invest years of their life in building up that specific skill set, at great personal expense, to accept such a poor salary? You would have to be hopelessly idealistic, determined to help those in need even if it barely paid a living wage. And willing to do that for one of the richest companies in the world, aware that their profits in 2020 were $86 billion and that they were being sued by former employees who had suffered PTSD as a result of the company's willful neglect. It looked like a non-starter to me.

I don't know if Zevo ever managed to fill that position, but it was a very depressing thing to see. I'm sure they were just working with the budget they had been given, trying to do the best they could for a client that didn't see any value in what they did and struggling to build a business on crumbs from the giant's table.

My feeling is that Zevo is as well-meaning and powerless as everyone else in this whole sorry story. The problem is systemic, not the result of malice or particular incompetence by any of the people I've had to deal with. We're all just doing the best we can in an impossible situation created by people in the ivory tower that is MPK in California.

THIRTEEN

GRIST TO THE MILL

I f you want to read the story that Jennifer O'Connell wrote after that first meeting, just search for my name and the *Irish Times*. It has a photo of me looking unshaven and slightly disreputable, alongside a quote about having to watch somebody being beaten to death on my first day at work.

It's a good attention-grabbing headline and I don't blame the paper for putting it at the top, but I never actually said that. It's a quote from a former colleague, Weird Alex – the guy who had given Jennifer my phone number in the first place. Alex joined the team about six months after me, and like me he had been drummed out in just under a year.† Since then he had been busying himself trying to find lawyers and reporters who would listen to his story, and he has also been diagnosed with PTSD.

We were both aware of Selena's class action in California. It had been widely reported in the press, but I hadn't considered

---

† I'm sure it's purely coincidental that CPL recruits new staff on 11-month 'temporary' contracts in a country that gives employees a lot of rights after 12 months in the same job.

doing the same thing in Ireland. For one thing, I had assumed that this kind of legal action was a uniquely American phenomenon.

Moreover, I simply didn't believe in PTSD. I had grown up believing in self-reliance and 'just dealing with it'. I hadn't yet made the connection between the problems I was having and this newfangled mental health fad. Selena's class-action lawsuit just looked like a cynical cash grab to me, and I just wanted to get on with my life.

However, after I left Facebook I couldn't make a clean break. For one thing, I hadn't been paid properly and was forced to fight for the money I was owed. Then there was the whole mess with my friend Maria.

As I mentioned previously, Maria and I had made SARs under the data protection laws to obtain copies of records CPL and Facebook had about us. (This was how I found out that my TL had proposed firing me because of my PTSD symptoms, and that it had nothing to do with my quality score as they had claimed.) This was a tremendously frustrating process because the DPC rarely replied to an email in less than a month and wouldn't acknowledge simple questions about what I was specifically allowed to ask for. Instead, their response was usually to just repeat what Facebook had told them and that they would like to close the case.

After nearly a year of hassle, I was frustrated and hostile towards Facebook when Alex called me and was happy to talk to a journalist about the way the company treated their employees. I was also intrigued when he told me he wanted to try to claim damages in court for PTSD. I had allowed the DPC to fob me off and had pretty much given up hope of achieving anything, but here was someone willing to try to do something quite spectacular. I was impressed.

However, as much as I like Alex, he would be the first to admit he's not especially worldly or good at getting things done. I call him Weird Alex because he's, well, weird. His brain is wired a bit differently from other people's and he sometimes has trouble with social interactions. He's also a terminal employee. He's not used to taking care of business and had been unable to find a lawyer to take his case. He was just spinning his wheels and getting nowhere, hence the call to me.

I did a little research as we were talking on the phone. Telling myself it was just a favour for a friend, I googled some personal injury lawyers and sent a few emails to test the water. I wasn't consciously thinking that I had been wronged and wanted justice, and I had no burning desire for a fight. I was just curious and pissed off, pulling on a thread to see where it might lead.

That was before I talked about the work with Jennifer and experienced that first terrifying public meltdown. Everything changed for me that day. Not only was I spelling out the sheer awfulness of the job for the first time, building a coherent picture and realising how much it shocked anyone from the outside, but I was also opening a Pandora's box of emotions that I had been keeping securely locked away. After that conversation, there was no going back.

All the same, I was still resisting. I had given an anonymous interview that was still unpublished and had received replies from a few lawyers saying they didn't think they could help me, but that was all. My emotional reaction during the interview was disturbing to me and not something I wanted to experience again. I wanted to give it up, drop the thread I was pulling, insist I was fine and just forget about it all.

However, I was also angry. Breaking down in a public place had been very painful and now there was someone to blame for the pain, someone to fight. Walk away from the problem or get into a conflict? Fight or flight? This is one of the hallmarks of an unhealthy brain and unfortunately that was what I had.

—

When the brain processes trauma, it sometimes gets it wrong and short-circuits the rational thinking part of us that says, 'I have this problem and I'm aware of these possible solutions', and defaults to a more primitive survival response, which is to either run away or rear up aggressively, fight or flight, no thinking involved.

When we have this reaction, the body floods with adrenaline, the red mist descends and we lose the ability to reason our way out of the mess we're in. Left to our own devices we just perpetuate this self-destructive catch-22 situation.

During this time the internet had given me, among other

things, a recommendation to watch a TV series called *The Bodyguard*. This was a thriller about an ex-soldier tasked with protecting a government minister – a great story – and also a commentary on what war and conflict can do to people. The central character was not an invulnerable hero, but someone whose personal life was falling apart as he struggled with mental health issues he refused to acknowledge.

Time and again in the show this likeable and decent person insisted he was fine when he very clearly wasn't. Left to his own devices, he would have been lost, but events and other people eventually break the cycle of denial and in the final scene we see him knocking on the door of the occupational health and safety specialist to ask for help.

It was a powerful and moving portrayal, and it was fresh in my mind as I wandered around Tesco in a daze immediately after the interview. I was at least open to the idea that maybe this was a real thing after all. If I had somehow released demons and ghosts, if something scary was happening to me, at least I had a name for it, a framework within which I could understand the problem, a defined enemy to fight.

I also talked to Dave Coleman, one of the leading personal injury lawyers in Ireland. I had no idea who he was when I emailed his practice, and he didn't reply immediately. He had gone away to do his own research, and around the same time as the interview he phoned me with questions about my life, my current situation and my work for Facebook. He seemed genuinely interested in me and I think he was the first person to explicitly say to me, 'You have been harmed by these people'.

I was still a bit dubious about the whole idea of litigation and claims for damages. It didn't fit with my stoic upbringing. However, somewhere in my research, I came across a government website that talked about litigation from a different angle. It stated that if nobody ever sought redress for wrongdoing then there would be no incentive for right-doing. The possibility of legal action is a deterrent to those who would abuse their power. It's also something that affects ongoing insurance costs. Take care of your employees and it costs you less money. Society had decided that people like me should seek compensation for harm suffered so that nobody else has to suffer the same harm in future. That tipped the balance, and I was convinced.

—

Between Dave, Jennifer, my long-suffering wife and a good pop culture role model, the number of voices telling me to go to see my doctor was too great to ignore, so I found the courage to make the appointment. Soon I was having another meltdown as I tried again to talk about some of the things I had seen.

At least this time it was in the privacy of a consulting room, with someone qualified to tell me what was going on. She informed me, without any hesitation, that I had PTSD and depression. It was official: something in my head had been damaged by my working conditions.

Addressing these issues was going to take time and money.

I didn't have an occupational health and safety specialist to help but I did have one of the best lawyers in the country on my side and a top journalist eager to tell my story. As she was putting the finishing touches on the article I realised I didn't want my contribution to be off the record.

Now that I understood what had happened to me, I understood why, three times in the year since I had left Facebook, I had got into conflicts that cost me my job. I understood why I had been pushed out from Facebook in the first place and why I still couldn't get a good night's sleep.

Even if I was not going to be well for a while, probably for several years, I at least had an opportunity to be compensated. I wasn't at peace, but I could see the way forward. It was all very simple: I had to fight the evil empire and join the rebellion.

The first blow I could strike was to break the power of the Facebook omertà that was still holding my former colleagues in thrall. I was confident by now, having done my research, that the NDA was not enforceable and, in any case, I would probably be protected under Ireland's whistle-blower protection laws. I believed I could speak publicly and Facebook would not be able to take any action against me in response.

Putting my name and my face on the story would hurt Facebook far more than any of the anonymous reports that had surfaced so far. It would publicly challenge their power and encourage others to speak up. It would make my story more credible, shine a light onto something they wanted to keep in the shadows and force them onto the defensive. Maybe it would even lead to reforms in the workplace where so many of my friends were still soldiering on.

I called a delighted but somewhat concerned Jennifer O'Connell and told her I wanted to go public. This was great news for her as it made the story a lot more compelling and newsworthy, but she was a bit worried that I might be endangering myself. I didn't care. I was blazing angry and needed to hit back at someone, as weak people are wont to do. If all I could do was stand there and be seen, then at least that was a start.

Dave Coleman was happy too. After our first chat on the phone, he came to visit me at home before I ever went to his office. We had a good discussion, and he went on his way, but I don't believe he was only there to get my business: I think he wanted also to scope me out, to get a feel for who I was and how I lived and to assess my suitability as a plaintiff. For someone of that calibre, the fees from my case alone would not be very enticing, not compared with the millions Selena's lawyers took. He would need to finance all of the litigation, possibly for years, until the case was resolved. I don't blame him for wanting a big payout to make it worth the risk.

So how would he get that? Ireland doesn't have class-action lawsuits like the US does, but the basic principle can still be applied here. Find a big enough group of people with the same problem, win a case on behalf of all of them, and the combined fees become very attractive.

The difference is that in Ireland we have 'group actions',

where lots of people bring similar cases and the judge agrees to hear a few representative ones. The verdict will then apply to all of them and any subsequent ones. My new lawyer needed a group of people to make individual claims against Facebook, and the best way to make that happen was to get publicity. However, it had to be the right kind of publicity.

If I had shown signs of being dangerously unstable, I imagine that he wouldn't have taken the case. I needed to be a credible witness, not just a troublemaker with a useful diagnosis – someone that could engage with the media and come across as a relatable everyman. Having determined that I was probably up to the role, he left me to it. I don't mean he abandoned me: I mean he didn't try to take control and speak for me. I had my own voice, so he merely advised me on topics and statements to steer clear of to avoid jeopardising the case. In the weeks and months that followed, we gave plenty of interviews together, very much as partners, promoting the message that it was okay to challenge Facebook's power and seek justice.

You might be wondering why I do my own PR instead of leaving it to my legal team as Selena did. Apart from just being angry and wanting to talk, I realised that a court case is like any other sale: it rests on your credibility. If I were the only one bringing an action against Facebook, it would be easy for them to portray me as a lone troublemaker. With fifty of us, it would be believable that there were many more in the shadows as well, afraid to speak out but relying on us to win justice for them. However, to get fifty, I had to set an example.

What I didn't realise was that by doing so I was also opening a floodgate of emotion that I would struggle to close. In the days and weeks following the publication of that first interview, I was bombarded with media requests from around the world, and I obliged all of them compulsively. I needed to talk about the things I had been repressing, and every interview I gave triggered another memory, another ghost that needed a voice.

I also had to respond to the many, many messages from people who knew me or had done the same job. My Facebook chat, email, LinkedIn and WhatsApp† were inundated with people congratulating me for speaking out and often sharing their own stories too. One message that stood out was a former colleague who wrote to tell me that they had left because they were really 'having trouble' with the content. I was shocked. This was someone that I had thought of as a machine, powering through the work without showing any emotional connection to it.

Just-protecting-my-quality guy also got in touch. He phoned to ask if it was true I was being sued by Facebook for breaking the NDA. His latest TL had told him and his team that Facebook wouldn't tolerate this kind of thing and that I was going to get sued to smithereens. I remember laughing with him about it because it sounded like what it was: a weak

† These were my remaining social media platforms at the time. I deleted my Facebook account later that summer as my growing self-awareness made me realise how much I hated it.

leader with nothing in his toolkit except intimidation.

I never heard a peep out of Facebook about the things I said about them in that interview or any other. Their only comment was the official statement they provided to the *Irish Times*, published on 30 March 2019, which I'm reproducing here:

> In a statement, a Facebook spokesperson said that content reviewers were not given targets 'for either the amount of time a job might take or for the amount processed on any given day. In fact, we specifically instruct our partners to not put this sort of pressure on reviewers.
>
> 'Some type of content, like nudity, is easy to establish and can be reviewed within seconds,' says Facebook. 'Others, like impersonation, take longer to confirm.'
>
> Reviewers are encouraged 'to take the time they need to make a determination', Facebook says.
>
> The spokesperson added that Facebook is 'committed to providing support for our content reviewers as we recognise that reviewing certain types of content can be hard, so we take reports like this incredibly seriously. Everyone who reviews content for Facebook goes through an in-depth, multi-week training programme on our community standards and has access to extensive psychological support to ensure their wellbeing.
>
> 'At CPL, this includes 24/7 on-site support with trained practitioners, an on-call service, and access to private healthcare from the first day of employment.

We are also employing technical solutions to limit their exposure to graphic material as much as possible. This is an important issue, and we are committed to getting this right.'

Later in the same article, there is also a statement from CPL, my actual employer:

In a statement, CPL said: 'We care deeply about our employees and take any concerns they raise very seriously. We provide extensive training and support to everyone working to review Facebook content, to ensure their wellbeing ... We are working to understand what happened here, and encourage these individuals to share their concerns with us directly.'

Read that very last sentence again. In August of that same year, after getting a professional medical-legal evaluation from one of Ireland's leading experts on stress disorders and mental health, my lawyers sent a formal letter of claim to both Facebook and CPL detailing what had happened and the effect it had had. In other words, we shared our concerns with them directly, as requested in CPL's public statement. There was no reply.

Meanwhile, I quickly found that talking to the media about my time at Facebook, and the threatened lawsuit, could be incredibly time-consuming. Every interview seemed to take several hours or even all day. All of the people I talked to were getting paid by someone, whether they were salaried or freelance reporters or researchers funded by grants. Everyone was getting paid except for me. I was doing it for my own reasons, but I needed to earn a living too.

The interviews were not only time-consuming but also debilitating. Many of them wanted a sensational story. They wanted to know the gory details and, at first, I was happy to oblige them. I had this weird compulsion to talk about all the things that I had never processed previously. It seemed like every time someone asked me for an example, I would remember something else I thought I had forgotten about.

I would sit down to talk about the job, maybe imagining I was going to describe a murder, and instead find myself talking about a suicide that I hadn't thought about since seeing it eighteen months before. There always seemed to be another story, another ghost vying for recognition, and I was just trying to give them all a voice, a chance to be heard.

I'm not sure it was truly therapeutic for me to relive these experiences but, looking back, I think I needed to acknowledge them, to get them out there so that I could process them and move on. Bringing my ghosts back to life was perhaps the first step in learning to live with them.

Whatever the benefits, in the moment it was often extremely difficult for me to have these conversations and I began to feel that I was in some ways just a resource being used by others to make money and develop their careers. On the whole, they were very respectful and considerate, but the fact remains that they needed to put me through the mill to get paid.

It wasn't just reporters. There were academics and activists all wanting my time and energy as well. They wanted to write papers about content moderation, raise public awareness, fundraise, lobby for regulation, you name it. Everyone had an agenda and everyone wanted a piece of me. I started to feel ragged, weary and maybe just a tad hostile.

I remember one NGO (this time an *actual* non-governmental organisation) talking excitedly to me on the phone about how they could help raise my profile, win support from powerful people, rally the public in support of our cause and all the rest of it. After a few weeks, however, it became clear their vision for the future included an end to outsourcing and the unionisation of the industry. I was getting sucked into a whole political thing that I just wasn't interested in and I was becoming increasingly uncomfortable. During one of our phone calls, my interlocutor suddenly had to cut the conversation short because they were running into a meeting with donors, people who they hoped would provide them with financial support to pursue their agenda. I remember putting the phone down and sitting there wondering what was going on in that pitch. I was the only content moderator they knew.

What would they say when the donor asked what their connection to this industry was, what expertise they had, who they were working with, and what powerless, oppressed people they were helping? The answers to those questions, in order, were me, me, me and also me. But when I told them I couldn't afford to keep giving them my time like this, and needed a budget, there was no money there.

They would speak for me, I could sit in the shadows and let them make it their literal job to represent me, but they wouldn't share the money they were apparently raising in my name. There wasn't enough to go round, they said, so I offered to help them fundraise some more. Why not bring me in to meet your donors? But they didn't like that idea either. It seemed to me they wanted to have control, for me to be a useful asset for their thing, not a partner. It was white-monkey land all over again.

Eventually I reached the point where the compulsion to talk faded. The turning point was the weekend I was invited to London to take part in a panel discussion at Mozilla Festival (MozFest) in October 2019. Mozilla is the organisation that builds the Firefox web browser, a non-profit devoted to a free and fair web, and every year they have a big hoo-ha for fans, developers, industry insiders and the like to get together and chew the fat.

I hadn't known anything about the event until a week before when it was mentioned by my new NGO friends. They were hosting some kind of small group session at the conference and wondered if I would be willing to attend if they could find the money to pay for my flight and a couch for me to sleep on.

That piqued my interest, so I looked at the website and was shocked to see that there was also a panel discussion called 'Moderator's Toll' about the impacts of my work on people like me. The panellists were two documentary filmmakers and two 'Mozilla Fellows', grant recipients who had each been paid something like $60,000 by Mozilla to spend a year studying content moderation. The filmmakers had been to Manila and interviewed various ex-CMs there, that was their job, and one of the Fellows had interviewed me at length a few months before.

I was gobsmacked and furious. All these people were building careers on the back of people who were being harmed. They were making money speaking for us and about us, but none of us were invited to be part of their expert conversation. I sent a short email to the organisers asking what I had to do to get invited to this kind of thing. I had a voice and I was determined to be heard.

I don't know whether they were delighted to hear from an actual content moderator, or just embarrassed at getting caught out, but they replied the following day and invited me to join the panel discussion. Instead of a couch and the cheapest Ryanair flight, they offered me my choice of travel options, a decent hotel and a pretty good daily stipend for the duration of the conference. It was a small win, but a win nonetheless. The white monkey was going to be an expert partner after all!

The first night and day were uneventful enough. I wandered around not knowing anyone or what was going on but enjoyed it all the same. Diane, the lawyer from Dave Coleman's office who manages my case, flew in for the day and we hung out together. We went to the NGO's group session in the afternoon and then Diane headed home. I found myself alone in London on a Saturday evening with an invitation to the Mozfest party on my bedside table.

I didn't go. Instead, I lay down on my bed at around 6 p.m. and stayed there for 14 hours fretting about what was going to happen at the panel discussion. This was a change that had crept up on me over the last couple of months: somehow I had gone from a compulsion to talk to dreading it. I lay there imagining how the interview might go, or not go. Over and over. I was fearful. The emotions that had overwhelmed me when I first talked about this stuff hadn't gone away or become easier to manage. It was quite the opposite. I had no resistance to them any more.

A few months earlier I had been able to sit with a TV crew and calmly describe what an assault rifle did to the human body at close range. Now I would find myself choking up at just the thought of what I was going to say, several sentences before getting to the gruesome bit. I was falling apart and tomorrow I was going to be on a stage in front of hundreds of people, plus a live stream audience.

I was hostile to those I would be appearing with, tired of others feeling sorry for me, tired of the victim narrative, tired of the industry that seemed to be emerging around that narrative and screaming inside at all those awful people who had done all those awful things that were filling my head. I was a mess.

The Sunday dawned and I went to the convention centre early, bags under my eyes and alone. I found the moderator, facilitator or whatever his job title was, the guy who would be on stage there with us to direct the discussion and ask questions. I wanted to ask him to avoid the gory details, not to ask questions about the specifics of extreme content, nothing that might set me off, but I struggled to speak. I kept choking up, tears in my eyes. He seemed genuinely concerned for me. He was obviously a decent guy with good motivations and anxious to avoid upsetting me. I remember feeling relief and gratitude but not being coherent. I just wandered around aimlessly until it was time to go on stage.

Suddenly, I was on autopilot. Getting miked up, agreeing on who would sit where, format, ground rules, all that, it was all easy. This was no different from being in a classroom. I felt confident and in control. We went out there, we talked and things moved along pleasantly enough. One of my friends who saw it all online later commented that I was very dominant on stage.

I think he was referring to a disagreement I had with the documentary-makers, who insisted on the narrative that the moderator's job is constant, relentless graphic images of violence. I had to explain that it's mostly tedium, with a lot of petty squabbling and just a sprinkling of blood and gore. A sprinkling is all it takes to mess you up.

We nearly got to the end without incident, until I stumbled and fell on the final straight.

The trigger was innocuous enough. A question was asked about the pros and cons of using human moderation versus AI and where a line should be drawn to prevent harm being done to humans. One of the Fellows on the panel started talking about policy and I lost my patience. I snapped and interrupted her angrily.

I wanted to shut her down and found myself getting increasingly upset as I did so. I ranted that we weren't there to talk about policy and that policy doesn't matter. Content moderation exists because people don't care what the policy says. They post what they like and they report whatever they don't like. Then someone like me has to look at it.

I could feel myself starting to panic. I was going down a path best not taken, unearthing more ghosts in public, but I couldn't stop. I was getting incoherent. I started to talk about images of dead babies, about arguments with my auditor about whether a baby was actually dead and the fact that by the end nobody cares about the dead baby: you just care about being right because if you make the wrong decision you might lose your job.

Then I choked up. On stage in front of hundreds of people. I was having a meltdown and there was nothing performative about it. I had come into the room that morning determined to avoid all those negative emotions, escape the victim narrative and focus on having an intelligent discussion about matters of principle. I wanted to meet these researchers and policy experts on their terms and hold my own in a reasoned debate, but, as far as I could see, I had fluffed it.

The audience lapped it up. There was a long queue of journalists waiting to talk to me afterwards. I don't remember much about the rest of the day. I can't tell you whether I was calm and detached or an emotional wreck. However, I got through it and arrived back home feeling like I had reached my nadir, the lowest point.

The thing about low points is things can only go in one direction from there. Something had changed, and things were going to get better. I was sure of it. I was right.

FOURTEEN

A LITTLE OVER-DRAMATIC

After I came back from London I resolved to be a lot more protective of my time and myself. It seemed to me that I had come to the end of that road – that I had told all the stories I could usefully tell – and that the balance between the need to talk and the need to take care of myself had tipped. It was time to stop.

However, the media requests kept coming and, even after making a conscious decision to take more control, I still wanted to encourage other moderators in a similar situation to take action on their own behalf. The rage at the way I, and by extension others, had been treated gave way to a more principled and political motivation. I needed to win my case to get closure and I believed passionately that bringing Facebook to court to account for their sins was right and essential for me if I wanted to ever leave this behind.

I had a lot to do and now taking care of my own well-being had finally made it to the top of the list. I started looking around in earnest for options.

I had visited a therapist after my initial diagnosis six

months previously but had not made any effort to arrange for any kind of ongoing relationship. Sitting there talking to a complete stranger about painful things had been hard and didn't seem very useful. I didn't have confidence in the process, and I wasn't sure that doing it every week for a couple of years was going to help. I had a very erratic schedule that made it hard to commit to regular times and, even if I could, it was also a lot of money. I contacted VHI – who had provided health insurance for us in the last few months at CPL – about paying for it, but they told me that the policy specifically excluded mental health issues.

I was too scared of the emotions and the cost, and it seemed easier to just go back to being a grumpy guy who wouldn't acknowledge that he had a problem.

After London that changed. I had said all I needed to say about the things that were torturing me and acknowledged my ghosts, and now it was time to tame them. I was ready to accept help and didn't care what it cost. Now it was a matter of finding the right person.

Life is a journey, and it takes time to go from not believing something exists to being fully committed to it, especially when it's something central to your sense of self and identity. I needed to go through a process of adjustment, of coming to terms with reality, before I could deal with it. This is a good point to talk about what my new reality was and how Facebook were thinking about it at the time.

—

Shortly before MozFest, in October 2019, an illicit recording emerged of an internal meeting at Facebook in which Mark Zuckerberg was addressing a crowd of his staff. At one point someone asked him if he had seen the media reports about the working conditions of content moderators and the mental health impacts they were describing.

He replied that some of these reports were 'a little over-dramatic', a line that was gleefully reported in the press and even made it into the High Court writ we would serve on Facebook a few weeks later. It seemed like a tremendously disrespectful and dismissive thing to say, especially when you have rejected these people's claims without even taking the time to hear their side of the story or examine the details.

What I found most interesting was the full detail of his answer. He said that, given the huge number of content moderators (he claimed there were over 30,000 at that time), it was inevitable that there would be 'a range of experiences'. What does that mean? There may be tens of thousands of people doing the work and not suffering any negative effects, but some of them may be affected differently? If that's the case, how could you then go on to dismiss them as over-dramatic?

If you're employing people and you receive credible reports of some of them being harmed in the workplace, you have a duty to set your own opinions aside and investigate impartially to determine the facts. None of us can be experts on everything, but not knowing about the dangers of asbestos, lead in petrol or second-hand smoke doesn't mean they don't exist. If large numbers of people are coming forward and reporting a problem, it should be taken seriously. Dismissing it out of hand because it sounds like criticism is unacceptable.

As I discussed previously, I had a very hard time taking the idea of PTSD from content moderation seriously. I've always been very self-reliant and dislike admitting any weakness. As part of the legal bureaucracy for our case against Facebook, their lawyers asked for my medical records. I had nothing to give them. I don't go to the doctor. Up until that point, there was never anything wrong with me that couldn't be solved with good food, a walk and enough sleep. The idea that I might have something as nebulous and threatening to my sense of invincibility as PTSD was unthinkable.

It doesn't surprise me that a healthy young man with the world at his feet like Zuckerberg would not be able to get his head around the idea either. The difference is that he has access to all the expertise in the world and is surrounded by people whose job is to make sure he does get his head around complex issues he would rather not consider.

What is PTSD anyway? What causes it, how does it work and what does it do to you? Perhaps a story from my past will illustrate what it's not and why it was hard for me to come to terms with having PTSD all those years later.

As I mentioned before, I lived in Taiwan for a long time. One summer evening in 2008 I was riding my big rowdy motorbike home from a teaching gig. I was on a wide city road just before sunset, charging along in my usual manner, and ahead of me a little motor scooter was trundling along at the side of the road, carrying a woman and two small kids. The kids were not wearing helmets and ahead of them there was a taxi stopped by the side of the road.

There was plenty of room for everyone so I manoeuvred out to the middle of the road as I passed them. However, the woman on the scooter tried to pass the taxi as closely as possible and had nowhere to go when the driver opened his door directly in front of her.

I saw her slam into it and was horrified to see something flying towards me from the scene of the crash. It was a little girl – just a toddler – catapulted into the traffic by the force of the impact.

I tried to brake but it all happened so fast. She hit the front fork of the bike head first, then bounced off, ricocheting off the toe of my boot on her way down. I couldn't take my eyes off her. I remember looking down at this little crumpled form lying in the road as I slammed on the brakes as fast as possible.

In the handful of seconds it took for me to come to a complete halt and leap off the bike to run back, somebody standing by the side of the road had already rushed out and was scooping the child up into his arms just as I reached her. He carried her back to her mother. I trailed miserably behind, my guts tying themselves in knots.

Mom seemed to have broken at least one leg and was clutching the other child, who seemed to be unharmed. She held out her arms for the little girl and as she was handed over I could see quite a lot of blood running down her head. Thankfully, she started to cry and wriggle and we could see that she was conscious and not seriously hurt. Head wounds often leak a lot of blood but it looked like this one was going to be okay.

When I got home half an hour later, I parked outside my house and stepped away from the bike. I looked back at it and thought to myself that this was probably the last time I would ever ride a motorbike. I was really shaken up. I couldn't face doing the class I had scheduled for the next morning so I pulled out my little Nokia mobile phone and called the client, a guy named James Dean,† to let him know, and the reason why. He was understanding and supportive, and I remember him offering to teach the class for me, saying, 'If you need anything, I'm there for you.'

I was still standing on the street outside my home and just wanted to end the conversation because I could feel the reaction starting to set in. After hanging up I stood there indecisively for a while until I recognised I was in a form of panic and needed to talk to someone. Ten minutes later, I turned up on a neighbour's doorstep a gibbering wreck, babbling about what had happened. I told her the story, and she reassured me there was nothing I could have done. After having a good sob for all of ten minutes, I felt much better. That was it. Done.

---

† Most names in this book have been changed to protect people's identities, but this one is real, and he's a top bloke!

I had had a traumatic experience and my reaction was perfectly normal. Everyone I talked to was completely supportive and now I was putting it in perspective by dealing with it. I went home to my dog, who suggested we go for a walk up a nearby hill, where I sat under a tree watching the last of the sunset. Then we went home and I cooked myself a good meal. I was calm and at peace with the world, and the next morning, after a good night's sleep, I got back on my motorbike, rode uneventfully across Taipei and taught my class as if nothing had happened. I was fine. I had had an experience but nothing more.

This is not something I relive. I don't have nightmares about it, I'm not uncomfortable talking about it. I'm not traumatised by it: it's just something that happened, a cautionary tale to share with gung-ho young motorcyclists.

Compare it with the conversation I had with a former Facebook colleague just after I got back from London.

We were in yet another Starbucks, catching up on the gossip and joking about people we both knew. I noticed he was fidgeting. Something was obviously bothering him. He looked like shit as well. He told me he wasn't sleeping much and then shared something quite disturbing.

He lived in an apartment and had to take his rubbish down to the bin stores for disposal. One winter's night he was doing this when he heard a baby cry. He described the panic he felt. 'I just froze, Chris. I didn't know what to do. I thought someone was abusing a child ... like I knew they weren't, it was just a normal baby crying, but I wanted to go and kick the door down. Or call the cops ... total panic ... I ended up sitting on the ground in the dark, hyperventilating ... I couldn't think, totally lost it for a while ... I can't look at child abuse content any more. When they ask me to work that queue I make excuses and tell them to give it to someone else.'

Then he fell silent and just sort of stared into space for a while. Sometimes I do the same thing, waiting for the ghosts to leave me alone.

This was a confident, healthy young man speaking – someone who had never been through any particularly traumatic single experience. Something had happened to him over the course of his time working for Facebook that he was at a loss to explain and that Facebook still insists isn't real. I have heard dozens of tales like this.

I've seen this again and again: people trying to come to terms with a problem but not able to talk about what caused it. More than one person I know has started the process of bringing legal action but then pulled out when they realised they would have to talk about and relive the things that haunt them. They clam up, maybe because they're afraid of the emotions, like I was. Like me, they're often struggling to accept what the work has done to them. They contact me to tell their stories because they want to be heard and to be believed.

Content moderation is a different animal from what many of us think of as trauma, and I tell these stories here to illustrate how difficult it has been for me to come to terms with my experience at Facebook. It's hard to explain it to people who have never done it. Most people struggle to visualise the environment or the impact it might have; they have nothing to compare it to, and the best parallel I can think of is news journalism.

—

The American *Diagnostic and Statistical Manual of Mental Disorders* (*DSM-V*) recognises that journalists who spend a lot of time reviewing material related to war or violent crime may suffer PTSD as a result of long-term exposure, even if they're not personally present for the events in question. Fergal Keane, for example, a highly respected BBC journalist, resigned from his job as a foreign correspondent in January 2020 to focus on recovery from PTSD incurred in the course of his work.

It's sometimes referred to as 'vicarious PTSD' and it seems that content moderation carries a similar risk. Content moderators have even less opportunity to come to terms with challenging imagery because of the relentless workload and a culture in which they are expressly forbidden from having opinions.

The *DSM-V* was written before content moderation became a major industry or anyone started to pay attention to it. Even today, I can't find any independent studies on the psychological impacts of the work. None of the social media platforms have allowed researchers into the workplace or to meet with the people who are at risk. Remember the reaction from the Zevo counsellor when I touched on this topic back in the early days?

Claims from moderators such as myself have been met with flat denial by armies of lawyers determined to assert the unproven argument that nobody *can* be harmed. The class-action lawsuit in the US, the Selena Scola case, was settled out of court on the explicit condition that the plaintiffs accept that nobody had been harmed.

Facebook's official statements say all the right things. As I described in the previous chapter, CPL's statement to the *Irish Times* included this: 'We are working to understand what happened here, and encourage these individuals to share their concerns with us directly.'

When my lawyer wrote to both companies and said that 'this guy has been harmed by the work, what are you going to do?' neither of them even bothered to reply. Was I not direct enough in sharing my concerns?

Compare this response, or lack of, to the treatment of a journalist I met during an interview who worked for a news organisation. They told me that, twice in their 20-year career, they had gone to their line manager and told them they were feeling distressed about things they had seen as part of their job. On both occasions, they were immediately sent to the occupational health specialist, which is not the same as 'wellness' at all. Occupational health can send you home on full pay, arrange treatment at your employer's expense and generally take care of you. Facebook's wellness team can do none of these things.

In a workplace where the risk is explicitly recognised and taken into account, there is no stigma attached to experiencing trauma. When you're okay again you go back to work as if nothing had happened – in this case, the journalist had a long and rewarding career with no regrets, despite being traumatised on two separate occasions.

I've had many events in my life that were hard and emotionally challenging but ultimately no big deal. Shit happens, and we get over it. In the long term, these experiences shape our attitudes to life and our belief in our ability to cope with adversity. I assumed when I took the job with Facebook that, if I saw anything especially graphic or traumatic, the worst it could do to me was to knock me off my stride for a few hours and then I would deal with it, as I had always dealt with anything else that happened.

It simply never occurred to me that the drip – the constant daily exposure to awfulness – would have a debilitating effect. However, the insidious, combined effect of hundreds of small shocks every day, with no time to process them before moving on, was like running a big rowdy motorbike on dirty fuel that gradually chokes up its engine and reduces its power without you ever becoming aware of what is happening.

A murdered baby here, a nasty comment there, a dog being barbecued alive, a lot of evil, divisive rhetoric that you're not allowed to delete – it sapped my strength and left me perpetually exhausted and on edge. I used to feel that I needed to rein in my natural ebullience but now it had gone away on its own.

Like my former colleague who was triggered by the sound of a baby crying, I've found myself being caught unawares by several situations over the last few years.

One incident in particular happened not long after I got back from London when a friend texted to tell me they were on their way to visit a family member who had been admitted to hospital after self-harming. They were cutting themselves.

You'd think that if someone you knew sent a message saying they were having to deal with someone who was self-harming, you'd be there for them when they're looking for a bit of support. What did I do? I cut my friend off. I could feel a knot of panic in my stomach as I read his message. I'm a bit uncomfortable just writing this. You see, I know what it looks like when someone cuts themselves. I've seen too much imagery of self-harm, I've dealt with imminent suicides and had those 'Fuck, what do I do?' moments, and I didn't want to have to deal with this situation at all.

I pushed the panic down, looked out of the window, texted something along the lines of 'That sucks, hope they're okay' and didn't speak to them again for four days. I was focused on thinking happy thoughts, taking care of myself and consciously managing my emotional state.

Four days later the situation sneaked up on me again, and this time it could have killed me.

I had a couple of early morning chores to do in the city centre and was then planning to drive out to a hotel at the edge of the city to go to a training day. It was for mental health professionals and was organised by the Human Givens Institute, the people I had chosen to help me deal with my issues. Due to my public role in encouraging traumatised moderators to seek help, I had been invited to come along as an observer and learn what the professionals were learning. On my way into the city, I speculated idly about what the day might entail.

If I hadn't had those chores to do in the city, I would have been having those thoughts while driving my car, but Dublin is a traffic nightmare and I live close to the tram line, so I was comfortably ensconced on public transport as my mind wandered. What would I talk about if they asked me about trauma? I didn't want to talk about Facebook stuff. I was trying to leave all that behind me.

Out of nowhere, I remembered that I had cut my friend off a few days earlier. I realised that my 'avoidance behaviour', my need to keep away from a painful memory, had prevented me from being there for my friend. I suddenly wondered whether, if a friend and neighbour turned up on my doorstep a gibbering wreck because they had just been involved in a horrible accident, I would be able to be there for them.

I was horribly aware that there was something inside of me stopping me from living my life like I always had; and as I recognised and focused on it, I forgot to keep holding it down. I had given it life, and strength, and it came hurtling up from the depths like a vengeful panic monster that took over me completely. This was not the memory of seeing self-harm images: this was the memory of how the memory had affected me. Before I knew what was happening it had got the better of me.

I lost all awareness of where I was or what was happening around me. Everything went black for a few moments, and I was paralysed. I was gasping for air, lost, out of control. I guess this was how my friend felt when he found himself sitting on the floor after hearing a baby cry. It sucked.

Luckily, neither of us was driving our car when these incidents happened. If I had been on the motorway when it hit me, I would probably be dead now. Thankfully I was on the tram, and when the black fog cleared after a few minutes, I sat there with tears in my eyes wondering what the hell I was going to do.

—

By that point in my life, I was coming to terms with other symptoms too. The poor sleep, waking up feeling like I'd had a nightmare but not remembering any detail, cutting myself off from my wife and family, the flashbacks and compulsion to relive some of the worst images. Most of all, there was the hyper-vigilance, the irritability, the readiness to get into arguments with anyone about anything remotely threatening.

Just a few weeks before, I had got into a terrible argument

with ticket inspectors on that very same tram and held up several hundred people's evening commutes, all for no good reason that I can recall now. It was like everything was a danger, so I was constantly on edge and ready to defend myself.

So I texted the wonderful Sue Saunders, the therapist who was running the day's training session. It was a short message and just said that if she needed a subject to demonstrate her procedures on in the training then I was her man. I might have added that I was falling apart, but I gave no further detail. I asked for help and had confidence in the help she could offer, and then I was able to compose myself enough to drive to where I needed to go to learn about trauma.

So, let's talk about trauma.

One of my hobbies is sailing, and I've always loved the observation that 'a boat is safe in harbour, but that is not what boats are for'. If you're going to live a full and active life and challenge yourself to grow, it's inevitable that sometimes bad things will happen to you. Painful experiences are, as some people are very fond of saying, part of life. You just have to learn to deal with them, to learn from them and grow.

I've seen plenty of dismissive comments from people who seem to feel that the problems some CMs experience are somehow a failure on their part to grow stronger. If you're traumatised by seeing too many dead babies then there must be something wrong with you, they say.

They're probably wrong, but who am I to make that judgement? I'm not a medical professional and I have a very simplistic, layman's understanding of the condition, so nothing in this chapter should be taken as medical advice. If you think you may have some kind of mental health problem, don't look to me for a diagnosis. Go and see someone qualified to help you. The Human Givens Institute was a tremendous help for me, but, of course, your mileage may vary. Other approaches may work better for other people. All I can do is share what worked for me.

My understanding is that our senses connect 'you' to the outside world. Your eyes, ears, taste receptors and so on, are linked to your brain by nerves, and these nerves run through a kind of switching box called the amygdala. The amygdala then routes these messages to where they need to go: remember this, think about this, this is an experience, this is fun.

The amygdala doesn't do any thinking – that happens when the signal reaches the rational parts of your brain – but it is very much associated with emotion. And here's an incredible fact: these signals only travel at anywhere between 2 and 200 miles per hour; even the fastest messages travel three million times slower than electricity down a wire.

There's a gap between the amygdala receiving an input, responding emotionally and the message getting to your thinking brain. In emergencies, the emotional response is so powerful that it takes over before your rational mind has time to get the message, and then it prevents you from thinking. The rush of adrenaline, the panic, overwhelms the thinking being that is 'you' and suddenly you're a million years in the past.

The amygdala is an evolutionary response to danger. If something creeps up behind you, you need to react as soon as you become aware of it. If you take time to think about it first then you might get eaten. That's why we jump when startled. It's a survival mechanism we have carried with us since before the time of the dinosaurs.

The amygdala can react so quickly because it doesn't think. It relies on something called pattern-matching. All animals do it, and my favourite demonstration is with seagulls. I see them every day, hanging out on the banks of the River Liffey. They're quite fearless of humans and even famous in some places for stealing food out of people's hands.

However, when I hold my arms straight out at shoulder level, like a kid pretending to be a bird, the seagulls fly away. They might know, intellectually, that I'm just a human and worthy of nothing but their contempt, but their little avian amygdalae pattern-match and scream, 'Big bird! Predator! Escape!' So they leap into the air, look back over their shoulders, realise that they've been had and go poop on my car in revenge.

Some patterns are genetically programmed into us, and a lot of people flinch at reptiles because we're descended from creatures that used to get eaten by dinosaurs if they didn't give them a wide berth.

Many more patterns are the result of our experiences. When something happens that causes pain, the amygdala remembers it as a threat. However, it remembers the pattern, not the detail. When confronted with something new that matches the pattern, it triggers an emergency threat response before we have time to think about it. It tells us to fly away or be ready to fight.

It's a useful response in some situations, but in the modern world it often gets in the way. PTSD is a pattern-matching error. The amygdala is misinterpreting what it sees and sounds the emergency sirens. These sirens are so loud that they stop us from thinking.

In addition, most memory processing happens when we're asleep. This is when the day's experiences are sorted and moved into long-term storage (if they are useful). The amygdala is central in deciding what to keep and identifying the important threats to be vigilant for, so any error in the amygdala is going to make sleep a difficult and stressful time. I think I was waking up during this process before ever getting to the other kind of sleep – restorative sleep. This is when the body heals and is what allows us to wake up feeling refreshed.

This is all just an uninformed layman's interpretation of some pretty complex stuff, but it's an explanation that worked for me. It leads to a simple question: what are we going to do about it? How are we going to fix the error?

It's all linked to memory. If the amygdala puts a little flag next to the memory saying, 'Panic here', we need to remove the flag. That's not overly difficult to do because memories are not permanent. Every time we remember something, we retrieve it from somewhere in our brain and then write a new memory of it – a memory of a memory. When I was reliving traumatic experiences for the edification of journalists and their audiences, I was inadvertently creating a new memory of that experience coupled with a newer, more powerful emotional reaction to it, getting into a spiral of stress.

The Human Givens guys believe that you can interrupt that process and rewrite the memory without the little flag used for pattern-matching. You still remember what happened, but the amygdala stops panicking when it sees something similar. The fight-or-flight response recedes, and you're in control of yourself again.

Control is important. If you're a professional lion tamer confronted by a lion, you don't panic. You have confidence in your capacity to deal with this threat, to control the situation so that it's not traumatic. If you're a soldier in a combat zone, living in terror of roadside bombs, you have no way to respond to the danger, no control over your fate. Every paper bag in the street is a threat, and you're traumatised by your powerlessness as much as by the danger.

By giving people back a sense of control, by reliving the traumatic experience in a setting that doesn't relive the threat, the theory goes that you can break the link between the memory (or the memory of the memory ...) and the debilitating emotions.

—

The day before the incident on the tram I had sat in a room with a dozen or so mental health professionals and watched as one talked about her phobia of spiders. Then, in a calm, trance-like state induced by Sue, she was guided through a process to separate the idea and memories of spiders from the emotional anxiety.

When we stopped for lunch, she went into the hotel garden to look for spiders, fearlessly curious to know what it felt like to hold one in her hand without panicking. It was transformational, and I was eager to try and exorcise the demon that had just grabbed hold of me on the tram.

I can't go into detail about the actual process, because I'm not qualified to talk about such things, but I can say what the impact was on me. I was unable to speak in coherent sentences during the first part of the session. I focused on breathing, tense and sweating. As I had volunteered to be the test subject, everyone else needed to know what the problem was, but all I could do was hand my phone to Sue and let her read the conversation out loud. She knew my history and was able to fill everyone in.

Once I was sitting comfortably, we began. They call it 'rewind therapy', and you're not allowed to speak during it. The speech centre of the brain needs to shut down along with anything else not essential to the process, and so – thankfully – you don't actually relive the trauma by telling it all again. Instead, a skilled practitioner leads you through an exercise to put it to bed, to reprogram the amygdala.

Then we went for lunch. I texted my friend while we were eating and apologised for cutting them off. I asked how everyone was and was able to function like a normal human being again. I felt fine. That evening I called them again and sat up in bed with my phone pressed to my ear while we talked about mental health and self-harm for over an hour. I was totally fine and slept like a baby afterwards.

I had a handful of rewind sessions with Sue over the next year or so. The amazing thing is not that this kind of therapy seemed to work for me but that it wasn't necessary to go every week. I had my head around the problem now, and the therapy created space for me to talk about it without getting upset. Once I could do that, I quickly developed the self-awareness that let me recognise when I was losing my grip. I conquered, to an extent, my amygdala and got myself onto an even keel, but I can't say I was cured.

I'm in a unique situation, which is that I can't just put all this behind me. I suppose I could just sit back and wait for the lawyers to get me some compensation, however long that might take, but while I'm doing that tens of thousands of people continue to work as content moderators.

When reporters ask me for insights about how content moderation works or when a moderator contacts me wanting to talk, it's very hard to turn them away. My work is not finished and understanding that PTSD is neither inevitable nor terminal just adds to the urgency. With research, I believe it would be possible to create a regime, a combination of a working environment and support services, that would enable content moderators to do the work without lasting harm.

It would still be emotionally challenging and would change the people doing it, but that's true of everything in life that's worth doing. Content moderation is important. Someone has to protect the innocent and defend democracy, and if the costs to the people doing it were managed and well understood then plenty of us would still volunteer to do it. We could solve this in just a year or two if Facebook would just acknowledge the problem.

This knowledge has changed my thinking about Facebook and my mission now, which is no longer simply to win compensation for myself and others. It's to persuade Facebook to stop insisting that they know best and to start listening. As long as they refuse to listen, I have to keep pressing the message. I can't let the ghosts fade away. I have to keep on digging up things that I'm personally ready to leave behind me and keep reminding myself of everything I saw that turned me into a wreck of a man for a while. Despite my much-improved mental state, that's still debilitating. I keep hurting myself because that's the price of doing good in the world. I am willing to pay that price because Sue Saunders gave me the confidence to know that it's a price I can live with. I can do this and be well again. When this is all over I will be able to finally walk away and let the memories fade.

FIFTEEN

THE WRIT HITS THE FAN

By the end of 2019, I had been on a hell of a journey. The year before, I was 95 per cent happy and competent tour guide and 5 per cent difficult employee about to find himself unemployed again. Now I was 80 per cent happy and competent tour guide, consciously managing my professional relationships to stay employed, and 20 per cent unpaid activist. I had been through the fire again and suffered through a certain amount of anguish, but it hadn't killed me and I was stronger now.

Life was pretty good again. PTSD had stopped being this mysterious bogeyman and became instead something to manage and eventually conquer. I didn't exactly have everything under control, but I had a plan and could see light at the end of the tunnel. Simply deciding to be protective of my time and energy made a big difference.

The press still wanted to talk about what an awful job content moderation was, but my interest started to shift. I wanted to talk about why moderation had become such an awful job and the decisions and policies that had created the situation. The 'victim fights back against evil corp' story wasn't enough now: I wanted more.

More would have to wait, though. First, we had to serve the writ on Facebook and summon them to the High Court. Throughout the autumn of 2019, the drafts bounced back and forth between various experts with me double-checking that nothing was incorrect or misleading. Zuckerberg handed us a PR win with his comment about us being 'a little over-dramatic', and this made its way into the writ along with a catalogue of some of the horrors I had been exposed to, how they had affected me and what the experts had to say about it all.

One day, at last, we were done, and on 4 December the writ was served. My lawyers marched into Facebook's GC4 headquarters and handed over legal documents calling on the company to account for their actions. The claim boils down simply to this: viewing extreme content all day is known to have harmful effects, Facebook knew it was harmful when they hired me and hundreds of others and they had a duty of care not only to warn us of that but also to put in place proper supports to mitigate those harms. The supports provided were inadequate, Facebook downplayed the risks and people were harmed as a result, so now I was demanding compensation – and I was just the first of many.

For the next few days, I was kept busy dealing with the media. The fact that the papers had been served was big news, and everyone wanted to talk to me again. It was all very straightforward, almost routine by this time. I was becoming an old hand at media interviews, and in next to no time I was putting it all aside and focusing on something much more important.

—

Having decided to focus on my own well-being, at last, I was taking a break and hopping on a plane to Indonesia with the two most important women in my life: my mother and Her Majesty my wife.

It was really good to be in a different environment and out of contact a lot of the time. With patchy internet, I wasn't easily contactable and it was the low season in the tourism industry in Ireland – a good time to take a month off and recharge.

We had a full schedule planned and spent a couple of days in Singapore first before flying to Medan in Sumatra, where the girls had to visit various dressmakers. My wife's sister was getting married and it was going to be a big affair. My wife and I had never done the appropriate cultural ceremonies in her country, so we had unfulfilled social obligations there too. It was going to be a massive thing, involving several changes of clothing. Mum had a high old time being fitted for various exotic outfits.

Then we headed out into the jungle for a few days to see the orangutans at Bukit Lawang and to take my 76-year-old mother white-water rafting. From there, via Lake Toba, we wended our way into deepest Sumatra and the warm embrace of Indonesian hospitality. We had several days to kill before the weddings, and while Mrs Chris was busy taking charge of that, Mum and I got out of her way with an excursion to Barimun, an elephant sanctuary.

It's a huge tract of land, and the elephants wander freely during the day, so we had to go on safari to find them. They're perfectly fine with people, and Mum was delighted at the enthusiastic welcome she got from a little half-ton baby when we tracked them down. Even better, and quite by coincidence, there was a solar eclipse that day so we got to sit and watch the sun disappear in the company of these amazing animals. Best of all, at the end of the day, the elephants all come back to base, and the handful of lucky tourists who make it to this remote spot get to feed them bananas by hand. Mum was completely captivated; I think I could have left her there.

After the wedding, which was more of a chore than a party, we were all exhausted and Mum had to head home anyway. My wife and I were planning a couple of weeks on the beach in Bali so we put Mum on a plane home first, once again from Singapore.

The first leg of her flight, to the Middle East, was on a plane full of Chinese tourists. Due to being mostly offline for a few weeks, we hadn't heard about the new virus that had appeared in that country. We don't know for sure if that's how she got sick, but a couple of days after arriving home she was at the doctor with flu symptoms.

Nobody really knew anything about coronavirus yet, so he gave her the standard advice. She took it easy and took care of herself, but she was still laid low for nearly two months. Stubborn old thing that she is – like her firstborn son – she refused to make a big deal of it at the time but told me later that she barely went upstairs for the entire period. She slept on the couch, didn't go out and had no energy for anything. By the time she was better, the whole world was going into lockdown.

Tourism in Ireland was slow in early 2020 but I wasn't too troubled by that. The previous year had been hard and I had therapy to go to. It was during this period that I attended the course with the Human Givens people, and I also had several sessions with Sue that helped me to come to grips with my situation. So that was all good, and I was raring to go as March arrived and my schedule was filling up with bookings to take groups of tourists around Ireland. As talk increasingly turned to the new virus, Covid-19, I thought back to the SARS epidemic in Taiwan, which had happened while I was there, and how much disruption that had caused. This seemed to be a lot worse. I had a nasty suspicion things were going to go pear-shaped, so I did what I had once advised Maria to do: assume the worst and make the necessary adjustments.

When the Paddy's Day parade was cancelled and the whole economy was put into hibernation, I just shrugged. We had plenty of food and toilet paper stashed in the store room, we lived in a relatively wealthy, modern country with good social services and we didn't have kids to complicate things, so we really didn't have anything to worry about as long as we avoided getting sick. My wife was managing accommodation for international students and her boss insisted that she was an essential worker at first, so she had to keep going to work. I had plenty to do, so we were able to just keep calm and carry on.

The project that I had set for myself during the few months that we anticipated being locked down was to try and get a publishing deal. I realised that although telling my story was an integral part of finding closure, I would never be happy if the story was told, edited and sensationalised by others. There were too many other agendas, too many competing considerations and too many professionals trying to use the story for their ends.

Writing a book myself, telling the whole story from start to finish in my own words, was the obvious solution, but doing it without a publisher seemed like a non-starter. I just couldn't see that I would have enough time and I didn't know anything about creating or marketing the finished product. I needed help, and it was Covid that allowed me to focus on finding that help. It was a hard time for a lot of people, and I did struggle myself later on, but overall Covid was good for me. It gave me a breathing space where I was financially supported by the government's pandemic payments and nobody expected me to be sending ten job applications a day.

Instead, I sent email after email to publishing houses and literary agents. I created a writing sample and book proposal, which took forever. For days, and then for weeks, I scribbled ideas and comments on sticky notes and plastered them all over our bedroom wall. I tried organising them into groups, experimented with using different colours for different topics and eventually came up with an outline, a list of chapters and their contents.

Most of the people I emailed didn't bother to reply. The ones who did all told me very nicely that it sounded great but wasn't suitable for them at that time. I gradually lost all enthusiasm for anything. It was a dud. The lockdown was dragging on, I could see that it was going to be a long haul and I didn't have any more ideas or anything else to do with my time.

Worse, the courts were not operating normally, and Facebook didn't seem to be in any hurry to resolve my case. There was no end in sight to anything, and slowly I sank into depression.

It's hard to say whether this was depression linked to my PTSD or just the normal depression that everyone was suffering at this time. I think that if I had been less ... damaged, if that's the right word, I might have been more resilient to the challenges of being stuck at home all day. Or maybe if I hadn't been stuck at home all day I might have been well on the road to recovery from PTSD. Either way, six months passed quickly and I didn't have a lot to show for it. I was still not sleeping well and was finding it hard to stay positive. I gave up, admitted defeat and went to see my doctor.

Until that moment, I had resisted taking anti-depressants or any other medication. I had always avoided this as a matter of course throughout my life, but after putting my heavy drinking days behind me I also recognised that dependency was a bad thing. If I hadn't already been nearly teetotal when we came to Ireland, I could easily have slipped into alcoholism due to the pressures of the work, and I didn't want to rely on drugs after my diagnosis. I was determined to win through with a clear head.

Unfortunately, it wasn't working, and with nothing to keep my mind occupied I was starting to ruminate unhealthily. There was nothing else for it except drugs, so I went to ask for a prescription, and she gave me one month's supply to get me started. I took them as directed, went for my daily walks as summer gave way to autumn and found ways to stay busy, but nothing changed. The drugs didn't seem to be helping. When the prescription ran out I didn't bother asking for another one. I spent most of the autumn in bed.

I did have one flurry of activity, though, when a former colleague at CPL contacted me to share some internal documents about how Facebook was responding to the Covid crisis and work-from-home mandates. There, in black and white, was an announcement (actually a 'task' or work order) that, since some content moderating centres in the US were now closed and their staff furloughed, my old pals in Dublin would be required to do more of what was now called 'P-zero content' – the nasty stuff.

I tried to make sense of this. Why was the site in Austin, Texas, closed and Dublin wasn't? Was the danger any less in

Dublin, or was it just that they could get away with keeping the Dublin office open? Maybe more importantly, why did work-from-home prevent people in Texas from doing their jobs? I had done content moderation in my living room during a snowstorm; there was no technical reason why the staff in Texas couldn't do their work remotely. Why did Dublin have to deal with more rape and murder all of a sudden?

I remember smiling as I read the announcement again. It related to the P-zero queues only. I could see they didn't want anyone viewing extreme content at home, only in the office where they could … do what, exactly? It smelled to me of fear about liability. Keep people in a controlled environment with some nominal 'wellness' support and you could continue to claim they weren't being harmed by exposure to toxic content. Let them do it at home, unsupported, with the additional risk of someone's spouse or child being traumatised, and the potential for more lawsuits was much higher.

This was fascinating and I combed the documents to see if they had explicitly acknowledged the potential harm to content moderators anywhere, but there was nothing I could find where they admitted that the work was anything more than 'challenging'. The wording was careful: Dublin content moderators were classed as essential workers, at least by CPL, and were therefore required to come and sit in a crowded office all day during a pandemic so that they could be properly supported while they reviewed material that Facebook and CPL continued to insist wasn't harmful, just challenging.

I made a few calls, and I wasn't the only one thinking along the same lines. I learned that over several weeks in September 2020 a firestorm of complaints and criticisms raged on Workplace as CPL staff objected strenuously to being forced back into the office to do someone else's work. Someone sent me screenshots of some of the threads. Many of the people complaining had previously specialised in other types of content and this was their first exposure to the nasty stuff. Most of them were immigrants, with no support networks in Ireland, worried about family members in other countries, and they were financially vulnerable. It was a shit-show of the first order, and CPL made a quite exemplary pig's ear of handling it. I know because I had a front-row seat.

One day someone sent me a link to a big Zoom meeting, what CPL called a 'town hall'. There were several of these scheduled one after another, and employees were supposed to attend in batches of a couple of hundred at a time, to hear senior management address their complaints. The links were open access, with no individual passwords, so I was able to join and witness everything that was said. To avoid getting into trouble I will only repeat what *Vice* magazine reported about them on 30 October 2020 after someone else (not me) sent them a recording

The headline was 'Leaked Audio: Facebook Moderators Terrified to Return to Office During COVID Outbreak' and the article went on to describe how the CPL manager conducting the session repeatedly dodged questions about why the work couldn't be done from home, or why Facebook's full-time employees didn't have to come to the office. The manager had done his homework and gave a long PowerPoint presentation, which listed many of the questions and complaints that had been raised online but somehow avoided answering most of them.

It got worse. He had to acknowledge that there had, to that point, been five reported cases of Covid detected in the office but couldn't explain what the correct protocol was in those situations, for anyone. One listener, who had a vulnerable family member, asked, 'If I get the virus [while at the office] what should I do then? Should I go back to my home and put my family at risk?' He didn't get a straight answer.

I was rubbing my hands in glee when the proceedings were interrupted by a woman who brought me back to earth with a thump. She explained – to 200-plus people – that she was an immigrant and didn't have anyone in Ireland except her husband and young son, and now she was required to spend all day every day looking at images of child abuse while also terrified she was going to get sick. I'm fighting back the tears now as I write this, reading her words: 'I think every day, if I lost my husband, if anything happened to me, who could take care of my six-year-old son? Every single morning when I start, I work on child abuse and at night, I can't sleep, I am dreaming just child abuse.' I can't imagine what that would do to a mother.

Amazingly, the CPL manager seemed taken aback to hear these criticisms and concerns. It was as if they had read all the comments online, put them together into PowerPoint slides and somehow expected to be able to just talk over them without giving any meaningful answers. The whole point of the town hall was that people were afraid and angry. They wanted change, and corporate platitudes were not going to be enough, so the first of these town halls ended in no amount of disarray.

The next one, scheduled for immediately after the first, started late and was conducted by a low-level staffer. The senior manager had something urgent to deal with instead. The next ones scheduled over the following days were initially postponed, then cancelled after the *Vice* article appeared. There was some press reporting, and even questions asked in the Irish parliament, but nothing was done. CPL's content moderators trudged dutifully into work every day, some of them got sick, several contacted Dave Coleman to put their names on the litigation list and life went on much as before. I was disgusted. I had had enough of all of it, but what could I do?

My wife was in Indonesia while this happened. Her employer had furloughed everyone, and her sister had just given birth to her first child, almost exactly nine months after the wedding, so she decided to go back to Indonesia for a month. That month turned into six weeks, and, although she had come back to Dublin, she hadn't wanted to. We were getting on much better, but being confined in an apartment with me through the coming winter was probably not the most exciting option she had right then.

One night we talked about it and came up with a plan. We would put our affairs in Ireland in order together, pack up all our belongings and sublet our apartment. Then we would both go to Indonesia in the new year, for maybe six months. If you're going to be twiddling your thumbs you might as well do it in the sun, and there were a lot of opportunities opening up for online teaching. I could make a living and put Ireland and Facebook out of my mind for the duration of the pandemic, and we would decide what to do after that when the time came. It sounded like a plan.

Motivated once more, I started taking my daily walks again but found myself increasingly irritated by all of the cyclists who were riding on the footpath. They would ring their bells and expect me to jump out of their way. It was completely unacceptable, and I started blocking them deliberately. One day I got into a shouting match with someone, I don't think he even spoke English, and some passer-by had to step in and try to calm me down. This was enough of a wake-up call to make me realise two things.

One was that this was an unhealthy and over-the-top response. I was regressing. The other was that while I had been taking the medication, I had not been bothered at all by other people just going about their daily business. I went back to the doctor and she gave me a six-month supply this time. I had everything I needed for my trip, except my visa.

Indonesia normally allows people like me to come in and out on short visits without any fuss, so we had never bothered jumping through all of the hoops necessary to get a spousal visa. Now the consulate in London had suspended all paperwork processing, so when the government closed the border to foreigners due to the pandemic, I was shut out. We paid a visa agent to get me special permission, but the rules were tightened at the last minute, and I suddenly found myself with nowhere to go.

We had arranged for someone else to live in our apartment and packed our bags. Since the restrictions looked to be in force for only a couple of weeks, my wife went on ahead and I made the best of a bad situation by taking a plane to the Canary Islands, precariously navigating the restrictions in force there to spend a week on a sailing boat. I hadn't sailed for some years and was in need of a refresher course, so it sounded like just what I needed.

I slept in my hire car for a few days, did a ton of fun and rewarding sailing, made some new friends, then slept in another hire car and waited for news that I could travel to Indonesia. When the news didn't come, I signed up for daily yoga classes. I hung out on the beach, explored the island, bounced around between various Airbnb apartments, backpacker hostels and rented cars and generally lived like a bum for three whole months.

Honestly, it was a great time. By the end, I was sun-bronzed, healthy, relaxed and physically and mentally stronger. I had let my hair grow, rarely wore shoes and was largely unaffected by the pandemic. I didn't have a stable enough environment to start doing any online teaching, but I did get an email one day from Gill Books asking if I would like to write a book for them. It had all finally come together.

My visa for Indonesia came through not long afterwards and, after enduring a week in quarantine, I was reunited with my wife in Bali and we rented the beautiful little villa where I wrote half of this book. Every morning I would get up just after sunrise and go stand by my swimming pool dictating into my phone. In the afternoons I would sit in my fancy office chair and edit the morning's output while my wife did whatever it is she does on social media these days.

In between times we would visit friends, hang out in nice restaurants and spas or take trips to more remote islands for snorkelling and nature. I ran out of anti-depressants after a few months, but it didn't seem to matter and I haven't needed them since.

Writing had started to become a bit of a chore, and about halfway through I gradually ran out of steam. My mind was full of things I wanted to say – I was lying awake at night trying to organise them – but I couldn't get it together. It wasn't writer's block: it was avoidance. I was raking up difficult memories that were sapping my energy. I was on a writing retreat on paradise island and I was tired, irritable and teetering on the edge of depression again.

In addition, we had overstayed our original plan and were paying for an apartment in Dublin that our tenants had just vacated. The Covid vaccine rollout was under way in Ireland, but Indonesia wasn't giving any to foreigners. It made sense to put the book on the back-burner for a while, return home, find a job and try to settle back into normal life, all of which were surprisingly easy.

Six months later, after a bit of a hiatus, while I got my thoughts in order, I'm finishing up this book and paying the bills by working 30 hours a week in a restaurant. I work for people who have everything under control and who provide the leadership we all need. It also pays better than content moderation. I'm still not sleeping well, due to the uncomfortable memories I dig up as I write, but I go to a yoga class four times a week and I don't worry about cyclists trying to kill me as I walk. There is no conflict, no uncertainty, in my daily life, I don't need to take control at work: I just let competent management take care of everything and do as I'm told. I don't aspire to promotion or worry about fixing things.

We're a mixed workforce, with proportionally more people of colour on the team than CPL ever hired. Many of the team are students, young and female, and they tease me about my 'dad dancing'. At least one has my number stored in her phone as 'Uncle Chris'. On the rare occasion that we get an awkward customer, they turn to me to deal with it, which I do by killing them with kindness. I'm practising compassion, for myself and others.

Facebook seem intent on making me wait as long as possible for a resolution to our court case. Maybe they're trying to wear me down? Whatever their strategy is, I have regained my natural ebullience and I'm still young. I'll wait. I'm in this for the long haul, and if it's going to take years then I'll wait for years. I'm not anticipating imminent enrichment, but all is good with the world.

—

While in Bali, I talked to a journalist who was doing a TV feature on mental health and I told them something that seems like a fitting way to end this book. I'm paraphrasing, but here's the essence of what I said:

> I'm going to be fine. This is not the end of my story. I'm not going to be defined by this. There will come a day when I'm not the Facebook PTSD guy. I'll never leave this experience behind me completely – I'll always have those ghosts following me around – but I'm going to make them work for me. I still cry when I talk about the work, but that's better than being numb and I'm better every day. I'm in charge now.
>
> Given the choice, I would prefer not to have had this happen, but it has, and it hasn't killed me so it's going to make me stronger. I need to win my fight to get closure. I'm going to win and I'm going to be fine. But Mark Zuckerberg will always be an awful person.

AFTERWORD

THE KEEPERS OF SOULS

You had to look, didn't you? All the warnings, all the tales of people being traumatised, all the discussion about how extreme content affects the brain and vicarious PTSD, and here you are anyway.

Take my advice and stop reading now!

'But Chris,' I hear you cry, 'if you don't want anybody to read this then why did you bother writing it?'

It's a good question, and one I struggle to answer, both to myself and my publisher. We're at the end of the book and we've told the story without having to resort to sensationalist drama, so why do we need to go into all the gory details now? It's not going to do any good and it might detract from the bigger picture.

These are all good points, and I do agree, but there's something driving me to keep writing. It's hard to put my finger on exactly why, but I feel like I'm leaving something important unsaid if I stop now. I asked Selena Scola if she understood and learned that she was struggling to complete the same exercise.

She started to talk about it but teared up in the middle of a sentence about 'meeting people in their final moments' and said something about families who don't know what happened to their loved ones. She described people like us as 'the keepers of souls', and I feel good about that.

People like us need to unburden ourselves and we need there to be a record somewhere. Here it is.

—

We can start with the dead baby. This was something I had forgotten about. It was in the context of Myanmar. We were seeing a lot of content about ethnic cleansing, the genocide, the stuff that was happening there, and somebody had put together a mosaic of images: burnt villages, starving refugees walking through the jungle carrying everything they own, injuries inflicted on people. One of the images was a baby lying on its back, eyes closed and not moving. Its hands were flat on the ground and there was an adult foot on the baby's chest. It seemed to me that somebody had stepped on this baby's chest and stopped it from breathing.

I took whatever the appropriate action was for an image of a violent death but my auditor disagreed. They asked how I knew the baby was dead. I pointed out that, even if you're a baby, if something terrible is happening to you, you try to fight it and push it away: your hands don't just lie flat on the ground. I think he accepted that argument and I got the point back, but that's all it was. A long time later that memory came from nowhere into my head. I realised then that nobody cared about the dead baby. We might as well have been grading potatoes. We lost the humanity. We were supposed to be protecting the vulnerable and helping the innocent but we weren't doing that any more.

—

Another one that I keep seeing in my head involves a group of black men. I'm guessing they were from sub-Saharan Africa. It looked like the video came out of North Africa, the migrant trail, where people were trying to get to Europe via people smugglers. I'd been reading in the news about black people being tricked into situations where they were deprived of their freedom and became slaves. To enslave people you need to intimidate and brutalise them. They were tied down in a room and a man seemed to be pouring molten metal onto the restrained men. I remember the victims writhing and screaming. It was really quick; there were no close-ups to see the damage to the body and no detail of what was going on, and it was just a couple of seconds.

I don't remember what we did with that one. I don't remember if it even broke the rules.

—

There was a video of what looked like a jail and people locked in a cell. A gang of men came marching down a corridor. The whole thing looked staged. One of the men reached in through the bars with a pole with a hook on it and caught a man's arm. He pulled his hand through the bars so that it was sticking out into the corridor and held him. Then another man who had a long pole with a big blade on the end took a swipe. I thought it was just going to cut the hand right off. I think it broke the bones, or maybe the man was seriously cut and it was still inside the sleeve of his shirt. Then the man with the pole jerked it up and down violently so that you could see the arm flexing in places it shouldn't flex.

—

A video of what looked like the Middle East showed a barren mountainous area. The camera panned around to show that a trench had been dug. A 10 or 12-ton army truck arrived and started offloading people who had been crammed into it. They were women, children and old people, not combatants. Men with guns shouted at them and lined them up along the trench. I knew what was going to happen but I had to watch it anyway because I had to take action on it. You have to take the right action for the right reason. There are so many different possible violations and you have to look for all of them. It's impossible to look away anyway. I didn't think about it at the time but now I wonder how that video exists. What happened there? Is it propaganda?

Sometimes we would see images and videos of people celebrating their victory, warning the other side that 'this is what's going to happen to you', and other times we would see people risking their lives to document what was happening and get the message out to the world. We're just deleting it because it might offend somebody, but if it is evidence of war crimes, genocide or ethnic cleansing, there's no button to press to say, 'Okay, I understand we don't want to show this to the world but we can't just make it go away. The world has to know.'

I guess this is what was so hard. We were in a room in a building with no external logo or anything to tell anybody what goes on behind closed doors, who we were and what we did. We were in the shadows just making stuff go away so that it didn't embarrass Facebook or the advertisers who don't want their brand appearing alongside something distasteful. We were burying the truth, hiding reality and creating a sanitised version of the world.

That reminds me of a photograph of what I assumed was the Middle East. A man was dressed in military clothing but you wouldn't know which army he belonged to. I have no idea what side he was on or what conflict this was happening in. He was celebrating, he had his gun in his hand and he was holding it up in the air above his head, along with a bandolier with ammunition, and he had a big smile. Behind him there was a half-destroyed truck or jeep. He was standing on a dead body. I couldn't be certain the person was dead, it might have been somebody who was lying down to pose for a picture or it might even have been voluntary. I don't know. He seemed to be in a big pool of blood.

—

I remember one day there was a big consternation in the office. It wasn't one of mine: I think it came from someone who was working on the Iran/Afghanistan/Pakistan market. It seemed to be a live stream from a village meeting. It was in the open and the whole village were assembled in a circle, all watching. There were a couple of old men with beards in judgement and men with guns. They had a young man in his early to mid-teens. I have no idea what he was accused of and what penalties he was facing, but he looked absolutely terrified. He was being pushed and shouted at, interrogated, and he was pleading. You could see the desperation in his face.

This wasn't surreptitious. This was obviously some kind of approved broadcast to let people know that justice was being done by some standard or other. Maybe it's some kind of Western bias on my part but when you've heard enough stories about honour killings and summary justice, and people being stoned to death, you just assume the worst about what's going on here and what's going to happen.

What do you do? This is happening now, this is live and there's nothing you can do. You can escalate material to the 'safety team' who have contacts with law enforcement, whatever that means. Maybe if somebody in Ireland was in front of a kangaroo court you could get the Gardaí to come and break the party up, but what do you do when it's in remote regions in countries where ideas of justice are very different?

I don't know what we did with that one. I think we just killed the live feed and left him to his fate.

—

I didn't see a lot of child abuse – most of that stuff was routed to a different team – but occasionally I'd get one. There was one that showed up with a man who had kids tied up with a rope around their armpits that was attached to the ceiling. They were half-naked. I don't think you could see the faces or the genitals. He was kind of showing off and had a cane. He would just gesture near them and the kids would recoil in terror; they'd obviously had experience of what that cane could be used for. I think there was a big fight about that, about whether it should just be deleted as nudity or escalated to a safety team. The rules were very precise as to when to take different actions. I remember several of us quite angrily arguing that it was abuse and that it was happening now. It was real and someone needed to look into it. Others just replied, 'No, no, it's just nudity, child nudity. Just delete it.'

—

The Isis stuff was probably the worst.

During one of the first interviews I did on camera this video came into my head. It was an execution. Somebody in an orange jumpsuit was unloaded off a truck and forced to kneel down. There was a man behind him on the right-hand side with a machine gun. He put it to the man's head. It was all staged for the camera, so it was from the side. He pulled the trigger. It's nothing like you see in the movies or the video games, where the whole head just explodes. In reality, it was like the right-hand side of his head disintegrated, but on the left the skin kind of held together. Everything burst away to the left with the impact of the first bullet. Then the tension caused it to fly back and it got hit by the next bullet, so it was flailing around, all one side of his head just flailing around. It can only have been for a second or two before the body slumped forward.

There was another one where they did it with a knife. I don't remember anything about it, except for that half a second when the head is pulled back as the body starts to fall forward. I could see inside the neck, like the black hole which is the throat and the oesophagus leading down into the body.

—

You don't always see the injuries. There was a car accident. I don't know why people want to post videos of car accidents. They put together kind of celebratory compilation videos of people getting killed on the roads. There was one, maybe in Africa, where a big pickup truck with a load of people in the back just lost control. I think it was trying to overtake somebody. It rolled down the road, and people were being hurled out, bodies flying everywhere at ridiculous speeds, with happy gangsta rap music playing over it.

In another video I don't even know if I saw the accident.

I just remember the camera kind of panning around the aftermath. There were people splattered everywhere, but there were no bodies ripped open. It was just lots of people lying around. I think at that time we didn't have the rule that if there was an accident and people appeared to be dead then we were to treat it as a violent death. I think at that point we were still allowed to leave things up unless they were gruesome. I left this video up and I got called on it by an auditor because I'd missed a man who had somehow been impaled on a fence post. I think it was a fence post: it was a metal railing along the side of the road, and the vertical post was stuck right through his body. He was face down and it was protruding out of his back. He was moving, trying to pick himself up with his arms, but not going anywhere because this thing was just stuck right through him. Again, what's the benefit of posting something like that? What kind of twisted individual do you have to be?

—

Sometimes people posted stuff with good intentions, albeit somewhat twisted ones. Occasionally there would be videos circulating on social media in China of what went on at festivals where people eat dog. There are some people who believe that the meat is best if it's cooked while the animal is still alive. One of these videos had been picked up in China and reposted on Facebook by somebody with the intention of raising awareness and outrage at what was going on, to try and get it to stop. This video showed a dog hanging by its back legs, still alive, and a man casually making ready to cook it. He had a gas bottle connected down a rubber tube to a big metal pole which functioned like a flamethrower. He lit the end to produce a big flame and proceeded to cook the dog.

A couple of years later I was in an airport somewhere and saw somebody looking at a video on their phone. The sound coming from his phone was of a dog in pain, whimpering and screaming. I felt physically sick just hearing that sound. He was sitting there smiling. I don't want to know what he was looking at.

There was a rule at Facebook at the time: you couldn't show cruelty to animals, except when it was in the context of food preparation. Dismemberment and the killing of animals were all acceptable if it was food. Since it was a dog and being barbecued at a festival where dogs were eaten, it was okay.

We were supposed to leave videos up if they were not in violation, but when somebody reposted the video with the comment, 'This is why I never eat in Chinese restaurants' it was no longer well-intentioned. The poster is not saying the festival is cruel: they're saying that Chinese people are cruel and that's hate speech. Or is it? Are they just commenting about what you get at certain kinds of restaurants? Someone has to make that decision.

Whatever the rules might say, awful people are going to keep posting awful stuff, decent people are going to use social media to expose evil and someone has to look at it. Whatever

THE KEEPERS OF SOULS

you think they should do with it – leave it up, take it down or hide it from certain people – they still have to look at it first.

That's never going to be easy for them and they're going to see things that will stay with them for years afterwards.

325

ACKNOWLEDGEMENTS

I have tried to be as honest as possible and to give a fair and accurate account of the events described in this book. I've also tried to tell the whole story and not cherry-pick events which give a distorted picture.

Content moderators spend their days immersed in a world of fake news, misinformation, interpretation, half-truth and spin. In time, truth diminishes in importance beside the quest for compliance. The best I can say for this book is that it's not violating. It might spark lively arguments about interpretation, but it's not going to get deleted, cancelled or censored. It will remain, defiantly speaking the truth that tens of thousands of content moderators labour in silence and obscurity every day, dealing with the worst of humanity so that you don't have to.

We are a unique community, permanently marked by the work we do, even when we are not explicitly traumatised. I owe all of them a debt of gratitude, as do you, for their ongoing fight in the service of decency, fairness and truth.

Closer to home, I want to recognise a few of the individuals who have directly or indirectly contributed to the journey I find myself on.

The moderators, my pals from my time at GC4 and The Beckett, all deserve a mention, even if they think they only played a bit part. People like Tom, Ariel, Jennifer, Ciarán, Chris, Nasrin and Leilen didn't get name-checked in the story, but they were right there with me for the duration, and I remember them all. Poor ol' 'James' gets less credit in the book than he deserves, and, likewise, I omitted the contributions of various people who did the right thing when asked: Lulu, Joeran, Wizam and Niamh. I also need to thank the ones I can't name, the ones who shared news and passed documents, my spies inside the industry who enabled me to sit in on group chats and read internal communications that Facebook and CPL would rather I didn't know about. You know who you are – thank you!

Despite my criticism of journalists and researchers in the chapter 'Grist to the Mill', some of them have made it their business to investigate, ask hard questions and get the truth out there with more zeal than was strictly necessary to sell advertising space. In particular, I want to thank Jennifer O'Connell at the *Irish Times*; David Gilbert at *Vice*; Casey Newton at *The Verge* and then *Substack*; Julien Goetz from France TV; Mike Wendling and Noel Titheradge at the BBC; and Alex Hern at *The Guardian*. Their efforts have made people squirm, which is a good thing. The team at Gill Books have been fantastic; especially Margaret, Djinn and Sarah. I have no idea how they've been able to read (and fix) so many words so many times, but we've got there and I'm proud of the result.

The wonderful Sue Saunders deserves even more thanks and appreciation for helping me to deal with all of this, not just the immediate trauma I came to her with, but the tribulations of reliving it all again and again as the public face of a campaign to win justice. She's been invaluable, as have the lawyers, Dave Coleman and Diane Treanor. Their support has been unwavering and much needed during the dark times. I'm deeply grateful for the friendship of Rae Jereza, whose research has done more than any other to shine an academic light on this whole sorry industry.

I don't have the time or financial support to fight the good fight full-time, even if it was healthy for me to do so, so I've stepped back in favour of people who can do a better job than I can. Cori Crider and Martha Dark at Foxglove in London continue to do great things for moderators worldwide: lobbying governments, building alliances and launching lawsuits on behalf of moderators who have been mistreated.

My lovely wife, who has remained nameless in this book because I don't want anyone stalking her on social media, has suffered stoically through this episode of my life. She has watched it eat me up, supported me through the bad times, endured my, ahem, behavioural problems and generally been wonderful. She has got me through it but there has been a cost to her. All I can say is, 'Thank you, babe.'